# Generations of Motherhood

## A Changing Story

*Enjoy my story,*
*Best wishes,*
*Lilly*

Lilly A. Gwilliam

Publisher: Generations of Motherhood Publishing, June, 2019
ISBN: 9781733899703 Book

Editor: Danielle Anderson
Typeset: Greg Salisbury
Book Cover Design: Judith Mazari
Portrait Photographer: EA Photography

To the loves of my life:

Patrick and Elizabeth, my two beautiful children—
you are my reasons for being.

Benjamin, Ashley, Emily, and Noah,
my loving grandchildren—
always believe in yourselves and follow your dreams.

# Testimonials

This is an absorbing memoir written by a strong, intelligent woman, who in spite of potentially soul-crushing lack of emotional and financial support, achieved a career dream she had from an early age.

Readers will relate to Lilly Gwilliam's quest to become the person she was meant to be. Instead of accepting setbacks, and repeating generational mistakes, she looked for and found solutions on her path to success as a mother, nurse, and in the legal field.

**Elisabeth Tuck, past president of The California Writers Club-Mt. Diablo Branch**

Lilly Gwilliam's memoir is a compelling depiction of a childhood dilemma that many of us have experienced. In it, she describes her own mother as being bereft of love and nurturing toward her as a child while demanding "entitlement" to love and affection from her. From that experience Mrs. Gwilliam explains the anxiety, anger and confusion that developed in her which negatively controlled how she lived her life. She shows a path from this dilemma marked by understanding and forgiveness leading her to push her mother's influences on her aside and to "become" a person free of her past and at peace with the person that she is. Don't miss Lilly Gwilliam's story. It is a story of courage to live one's own life with a genuine caring for oneself and for others.

**Maryanne Murphy, Esq.**

Bravely chronicling her path to becoming a successful career woman in her own right against many odds, Lilly Gwilliam tells her compelling tale of vision and perseverance to achieve her dreams, including a positive shift in intergenerational mother-daughter dynamics. Her struggle sets a fine example for all women who wish to break out of familial and societal expectations to forge a different path toward personal growth.
**Elizabeth C. Saviano, nurse practitioner and health care attorney**

Lilly's memoir is a powerful trip through the pinball machine of motherhood, life goals, and love. It resonates with women, but men should take a turn with it as well.
**Ginny Mattson Crispell, retired English teacher**

How brave Lilly Gwilliam is to put out her memoir for all to read! She is open and honest with her life and she deals with thoughts that many of us have, but do not have the courage to admit.

Lilly pursued her goals despite the obstacles that were there. It was not easy as she lacked the support of those close to her, particularly that of her mother, to help her along the way. On reflecting back over her life, Lilly said, "Life is not always tied up in a neat little bow." I think I shall remember these words, for how true they are.

From the introduction to the final page, I was engrossed. I did not want the memoir to end, wanting to learn more about this remarkable person.
**Lois Leonard, retired speech pathologist**

Memoirs are special. And *Generations of Motherhood* is particularly special because Lilly Gwilliam shares secrets from the heart. It is an inside look into the mind of this mother who examines with honesty her initial conflict, her trials and tribulations, her hopes for a better future, and the difficulties of forgiving. It took great courage to write this book. All women can identify with the conflicting emotions expressed on these pages. That is the one thing we mothers all over the world can share. Men and non-mothers can identify. We all feel the conflicts and love for a pet or a brother or sister or someone we love. In *Generations of Motherhood*, Mrs. Gwilliam shares intimate details of her conflict as a young mother, her hope to find her stride, and the difficulties of forgiveness as she grows older. This book is a keeper-definitely one you want on your book shelf.

Jay W. Macintosh, a California attorney/actress/writer, living in Nice, France

This deeply personal and heartfelt memoir is a beautiful testament to how one can persevere and realize one's dreams, while understanding and changing intergenerational family patterns, as well as challenging underlying societal expectations. In this compelling story of self-growth and deep inner reflection, Lilly shares her life journey of finding her voice, living her truth and following her soul's calling. Through this process, she consciously strives to re-create and maintain healthier mother-daughter relationships for future generations of her family. This powerful story reminds us that we can all come to a place of peace and forgiveness within ourselves, and with others in our lives.

M. Louise Cadrin, bestselling author of *The Starchild of Atarashara: The Field of Unlimited Possibilities*

Back in the 1950s, when all families were supposed to be like "Leave it to Beaver" with a cheerful stay-at-home mother, there were few children who admitted to something different. Lilly, the author, examines her childhood and her relationship to her mother and admits that they came up lacking. Those patterns, while regretted, are often inadvertently repeated.

Lilly, however, was determined to create a different model for her children. Here she tells the story of examining her past and committing to be a supportive mother while simultaneously managing to meet her children's financial needs and pursue her educational goals. It was a bumpy road---her story is that of many women of this era when professional goals were often not encouraged and day care was unavailable. If you are a child of the 50s, you will recognize a lot of yourself in this story. If you are younger, you will learn about and appreciate the struggle of a previous generation of women.

**Lynn Thomson Scott, Ph.D.**


Timely, intimate inside view of the tragic, long-lasting consequences of the early separation of mothers and children. Here, it's due to sudden, separate hospitalizations of both mother and infant, damaging the ability to attach in loving ways for each of them.

Fortunately, this is also the story of healing and inspiration. With lots of spunk, deep reflection, and psychological insight, Lilly Gwilliam shows us that even in midlife, it's possible to find freedom from early wounds and to experience love, happiness and forgiveness.

**Victoria Bresee, MA, MAR**

In Lilly Gwilliam's memoir you will discover a woman for whom even big problems are merely solutions waiting to happen! Whether building a family, pursuing multiple professional careers, or healing difficult relationships (especially with her mother), perseverance and ingenuity are recurring threads in this rich tapestry of her life, ancestry and aspirations. Her keen eye for detail will draw you into the world of her parents and grandparents while illuminating their influence on her, whether positive or negative. Lilly has written a story of courage, empathy and forgiveness with personal and universal appeal.

**Paula Wagner, MA, author of** *Newcomers in an Ancient Land/* **Principal Career Coach, LifeWork Careers, Albany, Ca.**

Lilly Gwilliam offers her well-earned wisdom in her memoir *Generations of Motherhood: A Changing Story.* As a child, she enjoyed the interplay of the generations, but grew up in an era where women didn't have a voice. Throughout her life, Lilly practiced pushing forward to new challenges with family, self and careers, and finds her way to success, becoming a role model of independence and compassion.

**Linda Joy Myers, president of National Association of Memoir Writers, author of** *Don't Call Me Mother* **and** *Song of the Plains*

# Acknowledgements

This memoir had been on my mind for years, and if it were not for my determination and the love of my children, grandchildren, publisher, writing coaches, writing group, husband, and dear friends, it may never have been written. I am so proud of all that we accomplished.

I want to begin by thanking my husband, Gary Gwilliam, for his love and support. He has been my backbone and allowed me the freedom to pursue my dream of writing this memoir for my children and grandchildren.

Another thank you goes to Julie Salisbury, who I met many years ago at a cocktail party during a San Francisco writers conference. We hit it off right away, but I was just getting my feet wet in the literary world and was not yet ready to be serious about writing my memoir. Julie and I reconnected in January 2018, and I decided to attend her writing retreat in Puerto Vallarta in March of that same year. She took an interest in my memoir, and here we are today! Julie, thank you from the bottom of my heart for believing in my story.

I want to thank my writing coaches, Linda Joy Meyers and Brooke Warner. I started writing my memoir in 2013 with the help of Linda Joy and Brooke during their class "Writing Your Memoir in Six Months." I had a lot to learn when I first joined, and I am grateful for my writing group in this class: Jean Rhude, Paula Wagner, Victoria Bresee, and Debbie Tripp. Thank you from the bottom of my heart; your feedback and responses were invaluable to me.

I next want to thank my dear high school friend Kathy Hanrahan Lawrence for her support. We reunited after our 40th high school reunion, and each time we have talked since then, she has asked me where I was at with my memoir! Kathy, you were relentless, and it was not always easy to tell you that I had nothing new to report. You were always gracious about my comment, but you also would not let me off the hook.

I want to especially thank my daughter, Elizabeth Phelan, for reviewing and collaborating on Part One of this memoir and I also want to thank my son, Patrick Phelan, for trusting me and allowing me to write whatever I chose in order to tell my story.

I thank my daughter, Elizabeth, and grandchildren, Emily, Noah, Benjamin, and Ashley for enthusiastically helping me choose the cover for this memoir. And, thank you Lisa Gwilliam, for your objective selection of the final three book covers. It was fun to have you all be a part of the process.

I would also like to thank Mike Angstreich, my high school classmate who nominated me to become inducted into the Massapequa High School Hall of Fame in 2014. Mike, I will be forever grateful for this wonderful nomination. Thank you so much!

Thank you to my aunt Judy Clements for being a great resource for family history. Whenever I had a question about my mother's family, you were always there and willing to answer. Thank you so much for your help and understanding.

Thank you to my editor, Danielle Anderson, whose expertise, energy, and adept knowledge changed my memoir into something that I am so proud to present to you.

A heartfelt thank you to my friends, Elisabeth Tuck, Ginny Mattson Crispell, and Lynn Thomson Scott, for your support and editing expertise in making sure my memoir was as close to perfect as possible.

I also want to thank Greg Salisbury for his patience and understanding throughout the many questions I had for him during the final stages of my memoir. Greg, you are a saint!

Finally, I would like to thank the rest of the Influence Publishing team for their hard work in making this book into everything I imagined. Without you, I would feel this memoir was incomplete.

# Table of Contents

# Introduction

We live in a society where mothers are worshipped or spoken of as if they meet every need for every person. However, for those of us who do not have that kind of mother, it's natural to feel less than others and to feel outside the realm of "normal." The wounds that we experience are real, and they cut deep.

I did not love my mother, and I worried about what this would mean once I became a mother myself. One generation of women impacts the next, and the reverberations are transferred from grandmother to mother to daughter. How do I change the dynamic and create a positive, loving relationship with my own daughter?

I did not get to know or appreciate the people my mother or maternal grandmother were as young women and how they felt about themselves; how they chose to become who they were and what family and societal influences affected who they would become as women and mothers.

It was not until I myself became a grandmother in 2002, at the age of sixty years, that I realized my children and grandchildren would never know who I was as a woman, not just as their mother or grandmother. By the time they may be interested in my story and able to understand it, I may not be here to tell them. I wanted to leave behind a legacy for them as I wished my grandparents had done. I also wanted to leave them with a foundation of how their grandmother, great-grandmother, and great-great-grandmother may have influenced how their own mother and father came to be who they are.

In 2015, a few years after I began writing this memoir, I was driving in the car with my son's two children and told them that I was writing this book. My eight-year-old grandson, Ben, asked what it was about, and I responded, "It is about grandma and how she came to be who she is today."

Ben declared, "I would like to read it!"

His six-year-old sister Ashley piped up and asked, "What is the title?"

"I don't have one yet."

"I think it should be about family," she responded with a smile.

I was touched by their sincere interest in my story at such a young age, and in this moment, I promised myself to complete this memoir.

I wish I could wave my magic wand and promise you that I had all the answers to becoming the "ideal parent," and that you will find them all in these pages. Unfortunately, I will have to disappoint you in that regard. What I *can* do is share with you my journey over the past seventy-seven years of my life as well as my thoughts and decisions based on my family background, all of which has shaped me into the person I am today.

*Generations of Motherhood* is about the conflicts I had with my mother and how I struggled to find myself and my voice and change the dynamic between me, my mother, and my daughter. I had to find a way to connect with my mother and have compassion for her despite what she had done in the past, and I had to let go and forgive.

However, this book is not just about my relationships with my mother and daughter. It is also about how I came to be the woman I am today. I faced many barriers as I pursued my dreams—my relationship with my mother being one of them—and I found a way to move past them and create the life I always wanted. I had to learn to let go of what the world expected of me and find the path the truly made me happy.

I hope that by reading how one woman overcame the

obstacles in front of her to fulfill her dreams, you can learn that it is never too late to become a better person and a better parent than what you experienced in your own family—that you can come to a place of forgiveness and peace within yourself and with others in your life.

# Preface

## The Conflict

In 2013, my daughter Elizabeth—also referred to as Liz—and I enjoyed a private dinner at BJ's restaurant in Elk Grove, California where she and my son Patrick were presently living. We always enjoyed talking and being with one another whenever possible. She worked full time as a licensed clinical social worker at a university hospital as well as being the mother of my granddaughter Emily, age eleven, and my grandson Noah, age nine. Her husband Todd was a stay-at-home dad, making her the primary wage earner in their family. Our time with one another was very limited due to her busy schedule, but we always enjoyed talking and being together whenever possible.

Today, though, our conversation was a little different.

I told Liz that my sister-in-law, Carol Ann, had called the ambulance for my mother, her grandmother, this morning. My mother was finding it challenging to get up, and as a result she'd been sitting in her recliner with a wet diaper for long periods of time. She had a neighbor who checked up on her frequently and had noticed she was having difficulty breathing. She had pneumonia and a urinary tract infection, and her legs and feet were so swollen that they looked like elephant legs—a symptom of her congestive heart failure, which she had been suffering from for several years. I'd last seen her two months ago in Massapequa, New York, and she had been having trouble walking despite using a metal walker. I knew that at age ninety-two this decline in her health was not a good situation, and I told Liz that I would be going back to visit her. Liz, as well as my son Patrick, loved my mother, but Liz had been informed of my mother's decline over the past two years and was accepting of her aging body.

As I was sharing this news, I went through many conflicting emotions. I felt annoyed, resentful, and sad. I had said everything I wanted to say to my mom, and I did not want to go back to Long Island so soon. I had been away at a seminar in Eugene, Oregon, for the past four days, and I felt so happy to be home. The idea of picking right back up and flying to New York was overwhelming.

The seminar I attended, "Personal Effectiveness," was intended to help you learn to say "yes" to what you want in life. It was owned and facilitated by my high school sorority sister Kris Anderson, and this was the first time I'd seen her since I graduated from Massapequa High School in 1960. It was wonderful to share her passion and be a participant in her seminar, which I felt would help me get in touch with my feelings as I began writing my memoir.

The seminars were intense, going from nine in the morning to nine at night. It was a very emotional and uplifting process as I was encouraged to look at my life and whether I was living in integrity with my values. The exercises involved sharing your intimate feelings with a group of strangers, although there was no undue pressure if you were not comfortable sharing your story. As a very private person by nature, this was a time of stepping out of my comfort zone.

During a one-on-one exercise with another participant, I shared the difficulty I had with forgiving my mom for all the negative messages that I received from her throughout my childhood. We had never been close since my teen years, and after years of therapy I unloaded all of my frustrations and disappointments onto her through various conversations from my late twenties through my early seventies. I struggled with my relationship with my mother and with my desire to come to forgiveness of not only her, but of myself. I did not want to have the dysfunctional relationship with my daughter that I experienced with my own mother, and that I had seen between my mother and my maternal grandmother.

It took me several days after the phone call with Carol Ann to decide that I needed to go back and visit. It seemed that my mother's condition was deteriorating every day. When I talked with her on the phone, I could hear the wheezing in her chest. She told me that she could no longer get up to go the bathroom, and that she had lost her appetite. She was tired and just wanted to sleep. My mother had been a very social person, so this was very unlike her. During one phone call, she said to me, "I just want to sleep and not wake up." I knew then that I needed to see her, and I felt scared that she may die before I could fully forgive her in my heart and accept her for who she was.

The impending death of my mother gave me a glimpse of what was in store for me. She was a relatively healthy ninety-two-year-old and had been active up until the past year. Now she had a difficult time breathing and often had to take deep breaths before talking, requiring the use of an oxygen machine to get air into her congested lungs. I saw that old age and increasing fragility are things we humans can't avoid.

As I came to grips with the impending end of my mother's life, coupled with the in-depth introspection I had just experienced in my "Personal Effectiveness" seminar, I decided that I wanted to be sure I was complete with my mother before she crossed over to the other side.

As Liz and I waited for our server, I mentioned to her how the seminar made me realize how important it was to have deeper discussions with one another from time to time. Life gets busy, and as a result we tend to keep discussions superficial and not talk about issues that are bothering us, which are then allowed to fester. What may start out as a pimple can grow into a boil, and then the boil needs to be lanced, allowing all the pus to drain before healing can take place.

Similarly, when we hold feelings of anger, sadness, frustration, and grief inside of us, we can get depressed and act out by drinking, taking drugs, or avoiding problematic relationships—whether they are with our mother, father, child, or spouse—instead of talking and expressing how we feel toward one another in order to heal and come to forgiveness and acceptance in ourselves and in the other person.

Our server arrived as I finished explaining this, and I took this opportunity to sit back and enjoy this moment. I was so grateful to have the kind of relationship with my daughter that I wished I could have had with my mother.

Once the server left, Liz leaned back in the booth and said, "You know Mom, I've always known that you and Grandma have a strained relationship, but you've never told me why. Whatever happened between the two of you?" She looked straight at me with her dark brown eyes, which were filled with an honest questioning.

I hesitated, unsure of where to begin my story and of how much I wanted to share with her. My mouth felt dry and my heart was pounding against my chest. Will she judge me as a daughter? She had fond memories of her grandmother and loved her dearly. Liz pushed her shoulder-length curly brown hair behind her ears, showing me her serious self that was ready to know the truth.

I took a sip of my glass of cabernet sauvignon and steeled my nerves. "Okay," I said, "but let me know if you get too tired and want to take a break." I then leaned in and placed my elbows on the table to get comfortable and began to share my story.

I told Liz about my childhood, about the ways that my mother had hurt me, and about the work that I had done to heal myself. We talked all throughout our meal—there were many years to cover. As I finished my story, Liz let out a sigh and shook her head. "I had no idea that any of this had happened between you and Grandma. Why didn't you tell me before?"

"I grew up witnessing the poor relationship between my mother and grandmother, and I didn't want to repeat this cycle. My mother has been a good grandmother to you and your brother, and I wanted you each to have your own relationship with her. And I didn't want to pass this dysfunction on to you."

I looked at my incredible daughter, and a smile grew on my face as my heart swelled with my love for her. "I am so happy that you and I have been able to have the type of relationship that I did not have with my own mother. I only hope that I was able to be a good mother to you."

Liz returned my smile and responded, "You were."

After we finished dinner, we parted ways and I returned home to prepare for my trip to New York. As I began to pack my bags, my thoughts drifted to my mother. Now that she was reaching the end of her life, I felt a desire to find some peace in our relationship. But was there still peace to be found? Or had there simply been too much that happened between us—too much time that had passed?

I finished my packing, knowing that there was only one way to find out.

# PART ONE

## The Loss of Mother-Daughter Bonding

# Chapter 1

## The Beginning

My parents met in 1941, when my dad was twenty-three years old and my mom was twenty. Eventually, my mother fell pregnant out of wedlock—something that was incredibly taboo at the time. Knowing that the other option was to face a life filled with the stigma of being an unwed mother and having no career aspirations of her own, she was more than happy to marry my handsome father. They married when she was three months pregnant, a fact which would not be revealed to me until many years later.

I was born at 11:15 AM on February 24, 1942, at Meadowbrook Hospital in Long Island, New York, weighing six pounds eight ounces. I was named Lillian Ann Radziewicz—Lillian after my mother and Ann after my maternal and paternal grandmothers. Because my father came from a family of six brothers and only one sister, he was so happy to have a daughter. In contrast, my mother always wanted a boy. I did not learn this until years later, but over time it became very clear that she preferred her boys over me. While this was difficult to learn at first, I now see that this dynamic actually freed me up to escape the dysfunctional family system and forge my own path, whereas my brothers were happy to simply follow in her footsteps.

After I was born, we lived with my paternal grandparents for six weeks and then with my maternal grandparents for seven months. My mother was the oldest of seven children, although at this time there were only five of them—her youngest brother Stanley, also known as Dopa, was born shortly after I was, and her youngest sister Beryl was born three years later. In fact, many of my mother's siblings were much younger than her; my aunt Joan and uncles Jack and Jim were only four to five years older than me. My maternal grandparents' house was small, and with so many family members living together several people had to sleep in the same room. The family dynamics in such an environment had to be stressful, but we stayed here until we were able to move into our own house when I was seven months old.

The cracks in my mother and my relationship began when I was very young. When I was four months old, I was hospitalized for a month with lobular pneumonia and came very close to dying. I have been told through the years how difficult my hospitalization was for my mother and grandmother due to the restrictions on visiting hours at the time. According to my mother, my father was fairly emotionally detached from me so this experience was not as challenging for him. However, I also think that that the relationship between my mother and grandmother might have been too complex for him to enter. I do remember my mother saying that my father lost ten pounds during my hospitalization, which counters the idea that he was not emotionally involved.

In May of 1943, when I was fifteen months old, my brother

Sonny arrived. He was officially named Stanley after my father, but we almost always call him by his nickname. While I don't have any memories of this time, I learned during a psychoanalysis session many years later that due to her pregnancy, my mother likely started to withdraw from me emotionally around Thanksgiving of 1942, when I was nine months old. As a result, a darkness would cloud my mood every Thanksgiving, and I would just want to be alone. When I became an adult and entered relationships with men, I would unconsciously break off these relationships at this time of the year as a response to these early years. Thankfully, once I gained this insight about myself, my feelings changed and I no longer felt the same sense of gloom.

According to my mother, she was taken to the emergency room due to a miscarriage for a third pregnancy when I was twenty-three months of age. She was critically ill and was hospitalized for one month; she was even given her last rites. This was another event that had a large impact on my psyche. It was a vulnerable time for me as I was beginning the process of trying to differentiate myself, like any child at this age. Years later, I saw a movie in my nurses training class that shared an observation made of children undergoing separation experiences between one and four years of age. It showed that these children had a sense of being punished by their parents through abandonment, along with experiencing a fear of further punishment and the loss of self-esteem due to a pervading feeling of "badness." This means that I, as the infant, would have been terrified of complete desertion, which would be in conflict with the anger I felt towards my mother whom I loved and longed for. Because of the egocentrism I would have had at this point in my life, I believed that my mother was angry with me, and this increased my feelings of worthlessness and sense of insecurity.

I cannot imagine how difficult a time this was for my father, and for the rest of the family. This situation was not in their control and they had to do the best they could at the time. I know that Sonny and I stayed with my father's parents, so he did have help and support from family during this crisis.

My mother has said that after she returned home and over the ensuing years I behaved as though I did not know her. I can only imagine how that must have hurt her as well. However, I later learned while I was a student in pediatric nursing that according to a theory in child development, at this young age I was repressing my intense longing and needs while also keeping hostile and destructive feelings in check due to this fear of further "punishment." My mother was unable to see beneath my mask and understand what I was going through, likely due to her being overwhelmed from her miscarriage and having two small children to care for as well as lacking this understanding of child development. As a result, my estrangement continued to grow.

As I look back on my childhood with the knowledge I have today, I find that I'm able to put a lot of it in perspective. When I was born, there was no blueprint or right way to raise a child and no book like *Doctor Spock* for young parents to read and become aware of the psychological consequences of child rearing. The first edition came out in 1946. In retrospect, my parents were doing the best they could under the familial and societal expectations of the time. It is because of this understanding that I view my relationship with my mother and father through a lens of forgiveness.

When I was six years old, Uncle Stanley died of pneumonia. I remember wondering where he was when we visited Grandma's family. We used to play together all the time since we were the same age, and all of a sudden he wasn't there anymore. I remember wondering what happened to him. Where was he? How could he be gone? This was my first experience of the death of someone close to me, and it was difficult for me to comprehend what had happened.

This was a very sad and traumatic time for the family. I remember my mother crying all the time. I did not know what to do with her sadness, so I would simply go and sit quietly next to her. I was too young to know how this loss affected our great grandparents and my aunts and uncles, but I do recall the tension and the uncomfortable conversations my parents had when we visited the house after Stanley was buried. My mother was very angry with her parents for not seeing how sick he was. However, I now wonder if she was blaming herself to some extent since she was often responsible for caring for her siblings growing up.

While I was too young to be directly affected by Uncle Stanley's death, I think my brother and I, and ultimately my father as well, were impacted by the subsequent emotional withdrawal from my mother. There was no discussion or talk about his death; we were each left to deal with the loss in our own way, or to not deal with it at all.

When I was seven years old, my parents and I went to live with my paternal grandparents in Hempstead, New York, while we saved money to put a down payment on our new home in Massapequa Park. By then, my grandmother and grandfather were sixty-three and seventy-three years old respectively.

I have many wonderful memories of my grandparents' home from this time. When I came in the door, I would walk up five steps to enter the enclosed back porch which served as a large pantry. I loved going up the two additional steps to the kitchen and taking in the wonderful aroma of Polish cooking. My grandmother loved to cook, and she would make delicious soups, soda bread, meat, and potatoes. Beets, cabbage, cucumbers, and potatoes were the most popular vegetables while kielbasa sausage, pork, and chicken were the favorite meats. Some of my strongest memories are of watching her make *golabki* (cabbage leaves stuffed with ground meat and rice), *pierogi* (small half-moon pies stuffed with cheese, cabbage, potatoes, or meat), and *nalesniki* (thin pancakes with jam or cheese). Meals usually started with a soup, such as barley, chicken, or my favorite, *barszcz* (beet soup). The soup would be followed by the main meal of meat, vegetables, and potatoes. Grandma always wore a printed dress with either an apron tied at the waist or a full apron when she was cooking. She would give me a half smile when I told her how much I loved her *barszcz*.

The kitchen was the place my grandmother spent most of her time, either cooking alone or socializing with her three sisters. They were all close in age and lived within walking distance of one another, and so they spent much of their time together. They would sit at the small table that was placed under a large window overlooking the swing off the driveway, where my grandfather and I would often sit and just be together. In her later years, my grandmother loved sitting at this table and looking out this window for hours at a time.

When my grandmother and her sisters were talking and gossiping, my grandfather would wave his hand up in the air, give a hefty sigh, and beckon me to take a walk with him. This ended up giving me the impression that their talk was silly, and that we had more important things to do. This influence kept me from joining the women's neighborhood coffee klatches that were so prevalent in the late '40s and '50s as I preferred to avoid any female groups that would get together and simply talk about one another. I believe my decisions to join professional organizations later in my life was my way of being with women who had a cause to work on together rather than have nothing to do but gossip.

When my grandfather and I went for our walks, he would talk about the time he spent working in Brooklyn. I realize now that my grandfather was forced to retire at age sixty-five, and by the time we were going for walks together he was suffering from losing his sense of pride and usefulness that he drew from being the provider for the family. At the time, though, I wasn't aware of any of that. I simply felt so special to be with him and listen to his stories of being a proud man and father. I think the fact that I now love walking three miles every day and have done so for years is a result of this happy and special time with my grandfather.

Across from the kitchen was a bathroom with a small window above the sink, a toilet, and a white porcelain bathtub that had four curved metal legs protruding from the bottom. I remember my mother washing my head over this sink when I got head lice from another classmate in first grade. She was matter of fact about the situation, but I was freaked out that these little critters were in my hair.

Beyond the kitchen, there was a small room with a sofa bed that had a large window above it, and in the winter the sun would shine on me and keep me warm as I sat and read. I used to love doing my homework in this room because it was in the middle of the house, and I felt as if I could be a part of everything that was going on around me. I liked hearing my grandfather listening to the Polish polka on the radio, which was located in the small living room toward the front of the house. I also liked to watch my grandpa enjoy wrestling on TV when it first came out in the late '40s—he was so gentle, and I could not understand why he enjoyed such a violent sport. I simply accepted that this was something that grownups found fun to watch.

In the living room, a chair and a small embroidered sofa with wooden legs looked across the room at the large photo of my uncle Joe on his bike. I had never met him as he died well before I was born. When my father was a teenager, he and his friends went swimming in a quarry and his brother Joe tagged along. According to what I have been told, my father went back home for a forgotten object and returned to find that his brother had gone into the water and drowned at only eighteen years old. This was the second child that had died in his family, the first one being a child that his parents had lost in Poland before moving to the United States. The family was devastated by the loss, but despite having this photo of Joe on prominent display they never seemed to talk about him.

To the right of this room was the bedroom where my father and mother slept, and where my grandfather would spend his last year before he died. Next door was the bedroom my grandmother would sleep in during this year, and there was another bedroom situated behind my grandfather's along with the one bathroom in the house. In the front of the house, beyond the living room, was an enclosed porch that my brother and I slept in.

Around this time, I loved to play with my porcelain dolls. I would place the six of them in a row as if they were in school and play teacher. I would talk to them and ask questions about their math and spelling. I remember disciplining my dolls for being late for class or not listening to me and noticing my grandparents watching me through the two small windows in the porch door. I felt embarrassed at first, but that feeling passed when I saw their loving smiles. I believe that the love I felt from them in this moment encouraged me to become a nursing instructor years later.

I remember that whenever I felt upset with my mother, I would go to my paternal grandparents for support and protection, unintentionally supporting a conflict that I didn't know existed. In a phone conversation with my mother years later, she said she had "wanted [her] own kitchen," meaning that she wanted more autonomy from my paternal grandmother.

During this time, my mother went to work in a shoe factory and was gone a good part of the day. I started to become ill frequently with "stomach aches" that were undoubtedly caused by separation anxiety, but I was too young to understand the pain I was feeling. My mother responded by taking me to several doctors, but the root cause of the problem was not discovered. I actually loved school, but I would still wake up in the morning dreading the day and wanting to stay home with my grandparents. After my parents left for work, I would go to my grandparents and say that I could not go to school because of my stomach aches, and they would let me stay home. This further amplified the conflict between my mother and my grandmother.

While I enjoyed being at school, my journey to get there could be less than pleasant. I was a chubby seven-year-old, and some of the kids at the bus stop teased me about being pregnant. Today, this would be called bullying. I felt self-conscious and became afraid to walk the block to the bus stop by myself, so my grandfather began walking with me. I felt protected by him because the kids did not say anything to me when he was around. In looking back at this emotional time in my life, I can see that the bullying may have had a greater effect on me than I, or my family, realized. I became obsessed with my weight for many years to come, although this was also influenced by my mother's struggles with her own weight and self-image.

My mother was a fairly attractive woman, but as a teenager

she had been about twenty pounds overweight and became heavier at different times in her life. She also had psoriasis—patches of dry, scaly skin—on her arms that often broke out when she was under stress, and she was always self-conscious. When I was a child she reached a weight of over two hundred pounds. I was affected by her constant need to diet and exposure to how her weight made her feel about herself. Then, one day my mother said, "You know, Aunt Edna told me that you are going to be heavy like me." I was about ten years old, and I found her comment to be hurtful and could not understand why she would share this with me. I never again looked at my aunt in the same way. I became determined to never end up looking like my mother. I remain weight conscious until this day. Even though I am of normal weight, I feel as if I am never thin enough.

Unfortunately, this negative influence would go on to impact my daughter. When I was a young mother, I too was obsessed with my weight and would never allow myself to be more than twenty pounds overweight. I was conscious of my daughter's weight throughout her childhood and even brought her to Weight Watchers with me when she was only about eight years of age. I unconsciously gave her a sense of low self-esteem and a feeling that she was not good enough as she was. I repeated the behavior of my mother with my own daughter, and I deeply regret creating this psychological pain in her.

Liz, on the other hand, has definitely changed this dynamic with her own daughter, Emily, who is now sixteen years of age. Liz does not impose any food restrictions or have diet discussions with her at all. As a result, Emily has a positive sense of herself as a young woman and has a healthy lifestyle.

Generations of Motherhood

Maternal
Grandparents

Paternal grandparents and uncle Julie

Mother and Father

Mother and Grandmother

Lilly (me)

Lilly (me) with Sonny

Liz and Emily

# Chapter 2

## Growing up in Massapequa Park

When it came time for my family to move into our new home, I didn't want to go. I was so sad to leave the protection of my grandparents and worried that I would no longer be safe in this new world that I was about to enter.

We moved to Massapequa Park, New York, in August 1950, when I was eight years old. After World War II there was a big boom of families looking to buy affordable homes, and many new communities were created to meet this demand. I thought that Massapequa Park was one of these new post-war suburban developments, but I later learned the community went back to 1696—only a handful of homes were built after 1900. Massapequa Park is forty miles east of New York City and only ten miles east of where my grandparents lived, but as a child it may as well have been a thousand miles away.

My parents wanted Sonny and me to be able to start at school in September, so we moved before our new tract Cape Cod house was ready and spent four months living with my mother's friends Aunt Mickey and Uncle Bill, who lived in the same neighborhood. They had two children, Lois and Billie, who were the exact same ages as Sonny and I. On Sunday evenings we would have family time where we would all sit around the TV and watch *The Ed Sullivan Show*, one of the few programs available at this time and one that we all enjoyed. Inspired by what we saw on the television, Lois and I loved to play dress up and imagine we were actresses. We put on a play for our parents and did a song and dance routine for them, and we thought we were pretty good.

This arrangement could also stressful at times due to the crowded conditions in the small two-bedroom home, but since we would only be there for a short time my parents thought it was a worthwhile sacrifice.

We moved into our newly-built home as soon as it was livable. It was a two-bedroom, one-bath home with a small kitchen, a living room, and an open-car garage called a carport. There was also the option of building additional rooms on the upper floor in the attic. The streets were covered with mud when we moved in, and it was not until the spring that the grass seeds could be planted.

The area we lived in was like one big family, with lots of families with children and no one bothering to lock their doors. We could head out on our bicycles to visit friends who lived blocks away without fear. We were outside all the time, playing jump rope and hopscotch on the sidewalks and in the street. In the summer we would make forts out of blankets in our back yard and read comic books. Of course there were days of complete boredom, especially during the times we weren't in school, but my parents would not listen to any complaints. This meant that I learned early on how to deal with boredom by finding something enjoyable to do with my time, such as reading—an activity that I still love today.

I have so many memories of my life in this house, and I am happy that I have been able to come back and revisit over the years since the house is now owned by my sister-in-law, Carol Ann. It had been a place to ground myself and to measure my growth as a woman. It is also a place of confronting my mortality because many of the people I once knew growing up here are now deceased. I cannot escape my awareness that life is truly short, and that our memories are a valuable way to keep our loved ones forever in our hearts.

When I was nine years old, I was in my room listening to a radio program when the announcer came on and said you could win free storm windows for your home by naming the tune they were playing. I knew the song, so I called the number and I won! I was so excited. I ran to the kitchen to tell my dad the news. He seemed pleased, but I don't think he was quite sure what to make of what I was telling him until I gave him the phone number to set up an appointment for the installation. The storm windows are still there to this day. I was so satisfied with myself at the time, feeling as if I was helping to take care of the house and the people in it.

Just like my paternal grandparents' house, my memories of this home are filled with the many fragrances that could be found within. I loved the smell and taste of my mother's rice pudding and lemon meringue pies, which she made frequently. Another favorite smell came every Saturday and Sunday, when my father would cook bacon and eggs to perfection on our new stove. However, the smell that I loved the most was my father's pipe tobacco. Each evening and on Sunday afternoons, he would sit back in his lounging chair, smoking his pipe and reading the paper.

Not all of my memories from this time were happy ones. One impactful memory comes from when I was ten years old. I was sick and stayed home from school, and as I was passing my parents' bedroom to go to the bathroom I noticed some papers under their bed. Curious, I decided to see what they were. As I pulled them out, I quickly realized they were nude photos of women. My father took a lot of photos and even had a dark room in the basement, so I believe he must have taken them. I repressed this memory and kept this secret to myself, although I never looked at him in the same way again.

This experience, combined with the tension that entered our family after Uncle Stanley's death, began to get to me. I started dusting, and sweeping our house daily, as well as my maternal grandparents' house whenever we would visit. I recall my grandmother expressing how cute it was that I would come over and clean her house, but years later I was able to recognize this as the early symptoms of my anxiety disorder. Looking back, I think that if I were the parent in this situation, I would not think this was so cute. Wouldn't you want to explore what was going on with your ten-year-old child if they suddenly started repeatedly cleaning the house?

Coming back into the happier side of things, this was also a time when I developed friendships that still exist today. My best friend, Sharon Agnone, and I spent hours playing with paper dolls at each other's houses and riding our bicycles to the grocery store. One day we decided to bake something while my mother was not home, so we just took a bunch of baking ingredients and mixed them together. We felt giddy and silly and anticipated a disaster, but to our surprise we miraculously managed to make twelve perfectly-cooked cream puffs. Unfortunately, we were never able to duplicate this amazing recipe.

Another close friend was Kathy Cooney, a neighbor who was a year younger than me and attended Catholic school. We spent many hours playing Monopoly together in the summer with another neighbor friend, Jean, who was two years younger than me. Kathy and I used to cheat by playing banker and giving extra money to one another so we could buy up all the property and win the game, much to Jean's disappointment. Kathy and I continued our friendship throughout the years and both ended up in the nursing profession—I think this was partially because we wanted to absolve ourselves of the guilt of cheating in Monopoly by doing something good. Unfortunately, Kathy passed away of cancer in 2015.

When I was eleven years old, I entered sixth grade at Parkside School in Massapequa. I was happy that Sharon was in my class, and I liked school so much that I was awarded a perfect attendance certificate at the end of the school year. I was also chosen to be the class monitor, which allowed me to help the teacher with various school projects. The dress code in the 1950s for girls was to wear a dress or skirt and blouse while boys were required to wear a shirt, tie, and jacket. We still had a choice of colors to wear and the ability to express our individual style, so the dress code didn't bother us at all.

During this time, my feelings about myself improved dramatically as I had lost twenty pounds the prior school year after going on a diet program. I now began to notice boys, and one in particular named Bill Nichols caught my eye. He had wavy, brown hair and was handsome and smart. We had a lot of free time in the afternoons—we only attended school for a half-day due to the schools being overcrowded from the baby boom—so Bill would come over to my house so we could spend time together. We would go on bike rides together and take walks to the park down the street from my house, just like I had done with my grandfather. This was my first time having a "boyfriend," and it was fun. This sweet relationship ended with the school year since we were assigned different schools for seventh grade and lost one another after being exposed to many other classmates from other parts of Massapequa.

Unfortunately, while I was starting to come into my own and find some self-confidence, my relationship with my mother was further deteriorating. Her expectations began to conflict with me and my "ego ideal." Her adolescence had been an unhappy one due to her being overweight, having a low economic status, needing to care for her family, and not being interested in school either intellectually or socially. Her childhood was somewhat stolen from her as she had to fill the role of caretaker at home. Whenever I wanted something that my parents could not afford, my mother would say, "Look how much I have given you compared to what I had as a child!"

I felt both guilty and angry when she would yell this comparison to me. We each have our own life experience, and by putting her difficult experience on me she was dismissing my concerns. I was left feeling unsupported and as if I could not rely on her for any help.

Sonny and me with Billie and Lois

Parkside school 1954

# Chapter 3

## Best Friends

In 1954, I began seventh grade at Hawthorn Junior High School. I liked changing classes and meeting new friends. I especially liked that I was doing well in school, and I loved science class most of all. I not only had a cute male teacher, but I also got an A+ in the class.

Junior high school was when I was first exposed to classmates from what we fondly called "the other side of the tracks." Massapequa was divided into Massapequa and Massapequa Park by the "three streams," a large area of woods and waterways. Our house was in an area of regular, straight streets with no trees until years after we arrived. Many families living in the tract houses were blue-collar—policemen, firefighters, secretaries, factory workers, and dry cleaners like my father, although later several doctors and dentists moved into the area. In contrast, I met friends from the other side who lived in mansions surrounded by large trees on winding streets, with screened-in porches that overlooked beautiful flower gardens and built-in swimming pools. The families were professional businessmen, lawyers, engineers, teachers, and bankers. Massapequa had some real economic diversity, although it did not have much racial diversity. We were brought up in a protective bubble.

I was awed by my friend Sandy Wange's home and loved to go there to spend time with her. Sandy was the first friend to introduce me to a different social lifestyle. I felt accepted by her even though we came from different socioeconomic backgrounds. Because of her acceptance as well as the acceptance of other friends who lived in her area, I learned to be open to all classes of people without judgement. She and I continue to be friends to this day.

The 1950s were a vibrant and innovative time for those of us growing up in this community. A new organization was started by some parents to encourage kids from ages eight to fourteen to get involved in sports. It was named the 4M club, which stood for the Misses and Masters of Massapequa and Massapequa Park. They offered basketball, baseball, softball, and football, as well as cheerleading for the young girls. This was a wonderful organization that helped pre-teens gain confidence in themselves.

I became a cheerleader and played basketball and softball, which allowed me to make friends with students from other schools in our town. My father, who was a respected football player in his high school years, decided to get involved as a coach for the 4M club. I loved that he was proud of me for being interested in sports like he was, and I was so happy to share this interest with him. My most memorable moment from this time was when I was selected to be the pitcher for the all-star softball team. I felt the pressure to succeed in this softball game, and when we lost I blamed myself for not pitching as well as I could have.

While I enjoyed playing sports, my interest in them may not have been purely self-driven. Sonny was not interested in sports, and I was later told by a school psychologist that I was trying to be the boy in the family to make up for Sonny's non-interest.

In 1955, the 4M club started a "football queen" contest that was adjudicated by a modeling agency in New York City. I decided to have a professional photo taken and submitted it for selection in my age category. Although I did not win the title, I won for my age group and being a runner-up was enough for me. I got to participate in a Thanksgiving parade with the rest of the winners, where we sat in an open car with red capes over our cheerleading outfits and gold tiaras. It was a fun and exciting time, and I enjoyed the attention we all received the day of the ceremony. My life seemed to change after this event; I felt confident in myself, and other kids seemed to be friendlier to me.

The school provided Friday night dances throughout the school year, and I attended several of them with another friend, Susan Heald. She lived a few blocks away from me, and we would spend several afternoons a week watching *American Bandstand* and learning to dance to Bill Haley's "Rock Around the Clock," made famous by the movie *Blackboard Jungle*. Other songs that we danced to were Chuck Berry's "Maybellene," The Clovers' "Devil or Angel," Little Richard's "Tutti Frutti," and Joe Turner's "Shake Rattle and Roll." We wore saddle shoes and thick socks with poodle skirts and a sweater, all highlighted by my ponytail to keep the hair off my face.

When we were changing classes one day, I returned to my desk to find a note inside from a boy named Donnie Olesen, asking me if I was going to the school dance on Friday night. I was amused and definitely flattered. Donnie was tall and cute, with red hair and fair skin. I had seen him around the school but had never actually met him since he was not in my classroom. Being tall for my age at five feet, seven inches, I was also happy that Donnie was my height. I left him a note in my desk to let him know I was planning to attend, knowing that he would be sitting in this same spot while our class was in the gym. We attended several dances together, and we had a lot of fun.

By this time my social life was in full bloom, and I had discovered that growing up was so much better than I imagined. It was a time of awakening to a new sense of myself as a strong, independent, smart, twelve-year-old girl. Over the years I would often reflect back on this time to remind myself of how I felt, drawing upon this powerful self to get me through the rougher patches in life. I hope that my children and grandchildren all experience this feeling in their own lives, and that they never lose this powerful sense of self-worth.

As my social life blossomed, my relationship with my mother grew even more strained. She boasted to her friends about my "social success," and I remember feeling like an object when I was asked to give a run-down of all of my activities to her friends. There was no reward or recognition for my academic success, which was where my priorities lay; the emphasis was on the boyfriends I had coming over to the house. I was already beginning to feel as if my mother didn't support me for who I truly was, only who she wanted me to be.

Donnie would continue to leave "love" notes in my desk for the remainder of the school year and we became a couple after going to a few dances together. Our first date involved going to a movie with several friends, and I can still feel the thrill and excitement of sitting next to him in the theatre. I was unsure of myself and didn't know what was expected not only of me but of him as well. Halfway through the movie I felt his arm move up around my shoulders, his hand resting with a soft touch on the back of my seat. I was in heaven. I thought, *so this is how it feels to have a boyfriend.* We later carved our initials inside of a heart shape on a wooden pew in the back of Grace Episcopal Church, and the image remained there for years. In looking back, I can see that this was such an awkward time in our lives, and that I had so much to learn about love.

The summer after seventh grade, I attended one of the first parties held by my friends. Even though I was flat-chested, I really wanted to wear a bra like many of my peers. I convinced my mother to buy me one, and I was so proud to go to this party wearing my thirty-two double-A bra for the first time. We played spin the bottle, and when it came time for me to kiss Donnie, he noticed I was wearing a bra when he placed his hands on my back. I overheard him mention something about it to his friends, and I felt so grown up.

Donnie and I maintained our "steady" relationship through seventh grade and into the beginning of eighth grade, but we drifted apart when we started classes in our new school in 1956. Our old school was too small to keep up with the housing boom in the area, so they had built a new high school to help overcome the crowded classrooms. We were the first group of students to start at this new school, and we stayed there until our graduation in 1960. Donnie became our class basketball star two years later, and even though we were no longer together I enjoyed watching him play.

Soon after we entered the new school I met Bill Barton, who was three years ahead of me, at an after-school activity. He was a tall, handsome, dark-haired, blue-eyed honor student who was also a basketball star. He was my first ideal boyfriend; he was older than anyone I had ever liked and was more mature than any male classmate my age. He was a thoughtful and serious person, and he reminded me of my father. Bill would walk the two miles to my house to visit me on the weekends, and on days we were apart we would talk on the phone about our classes and how our day went. After the Friday night games, I would stay behind and wait for him to shower so he could walk me home, and I felt so grown up walking out of the gymnasium with Bill. I decided that I would no longer date anyone my age ever again.

My first French kiss was with Bill, and I will never forget the passion and excitement in that moment. Bill also gifted me my first present from a boy—a red cardigan sweater and a gold chain with a heart locket that he gave me for Christmas—and I was thrilled that he had thought of me. However, after three months of dating, our relationship seemed to fade away. Bill became involved with another girl who was two years ahead of me in school, and she eventually became his wife.

I next became involved with Al Swanson when I was a freshman and he was a junior. Al was a tall, handsome guy with brown hair and blue eyes. He was the only child of divorced parents, and his mother was the manager/hostess of a well-respected restaurant in a nearby town. He spent a lot of time in our home since his mother was always working. We were together constantly outside of our classes. We shared a lot of our teenage and family problems and were a wonderful support for one another. We went to movies, played miniature golf, and went to family dinners and events together. In his senior year of high school, Al was given a new blue Chevrolet convertible with red leather seats and he began driving me to and from school each day. It was so much better than taking the bus, and I loved my new status.

When I was a freshman, I attended the junior prom with

Al along with my childhood classmate, Sandy Taylor, as well as her sister and their dates. Sandy and I felt very special to be at this junior prom when we were only freshmen.

When I was fifteen years old, the news came that my paternal grandfather had broken his hip and was placed on bedrest. He apparently had fallen as he was going down the front steps to get the newspaper. Hip replacements weren't common at the time, and at eighty-two years old there wasn't much they could do for him. My father and his siblings would all come by and help my grandmother take care of him, sharing their time to help their parents deal with the situation.

I often went to visit my grandfather during this time, and it was so hard to watch him deteriorate over the next year. I felt so helpless as I saw my beloved grandfather slowly slip away. Al would often come with me for support, and I was glad to have him there. My grandfather died on May 22, 1958. I did not attend his funeral. I had final exams to study for, and I wanted to remember him as he was when he was alive. My parents allowed me this absence since they knew how close I was to him.

Years later, I read my diary entry from the day that he passed. It simply said, "My grandfather died today, and I know he wanted to die a long time ago." I wrote nothing about how I felt.

It was not until I was undergoing psychotherapy at twenty-seven years old that I discovered that I had an "unresolved grief reaction" to the loss of my grandfather. In essence, I did not acknowledge his death because I could not accept that he had died and left me alone in the world. He was my protector and I could not imagine life without him, so I went into a form of denial.

The effect of this unresolved grief was that throughout the

rest of my schooling, I had difficulty studying for final exams because they would fall during the same time of the year as when he died. I would hold an A grade level during the rest of the semester, but when it came to the final exam I would do terribly and bring my average down to a B. I also often felt sad during the month of May but would push on and ignore it. This issue was resolved by undergoing psychoanalysis for several years.

Al and I spent two years together, but as his graduation approached I learned that he did not have any intention of moving on to college. He wanted us to get married, but to me this was out of the question. I did not love him enough to get married at the age of sixteen; I was too young, and I wanted more in life.

The summer after he graduated, he met a former girlfriend when he went to visit his family in Maine. They reconnected, and when she became pregnant they decided to get married. I only saw him a brief time after he returned home to say good-bye. I was devastated at first, but I ended up feeling a sense of relief once he was no longer at our house all the time. While we were together, I had no time for myself, my studies, and my sorority friends. He would get jealous when I was not with him, and I was constantly explaining why I could not see him at certain times. I ended up developing three small bald spots on the back of my head that according to my doctor were caused by the stress of this situation. I had been trying to do it all, but now I was free to spend time with my sorority sisters and focus on my career goals.

Years later, in 2014, I was inducted into our high school's Hall of Fame in recognition of my individual professional accomplishments and my position as a role model to the students. Donnie Olesen was inducted several years before me, and Bill Nichols was inducted in 2017. We, along with several other close friends, were among two hundred other inductees, including distinguished members such as Alec Baldwin and Ron Kovac. It is a wonderful group to be associated with.

I think our early life relationships have more of an influence on us than we think. It is not until we get older that we can reflect on our lives and appreciate the impact we had on one another. They serve as a barometer as to where we were and how far we have come emotionally, physically, and spiritually. My childhood friendships and relationships gave me a sense of belonging and a belief that I was good enough to be a part of their lives. They, along with my teachers, influenced me to continue on to higher education and seek a professional life that I may not have otherwise achieved. It is a gift that I have been able to reconnect with my childhood friends and come to appreciate who we have become as adults.

Cheerleading with 4M club 1955

Lilly at age 12 yrs for the 4M football queen runner-up

Lilly, center, at her first prom as a freshman in high school with Al Swanson, a junior, along with Sandy Taylor and her sister and dates. 1957

Lilly and her 7th grade boyfriend, Donny Olesen, at their 50th MHS Reunion in 2010

Al and me in 1957 at my first prom

# Chapter 4

## My Teen Angst

When I was in my teens, the conversations that existed between my mother and me mostly involved her talking and my listening. When I came home from school activities, she would be waiting to tell me about her problems, both past and present. She would go into great detail about her past experiences with dating and encourage me not to make the same mistakes she had. However, she often gave conflicting messages, one moment saying "Be careful that you don't get hurt like I did; never trust any man," and the next moment encouraging me to "Have a good time!" These double-edged messages eventually gave me the impression that she didn't want me to be like her, but that I shouldn't dare to be different either.

One of the most fracturing moments of our relationship came when I was sixteen years old. My mother stopped me as I came in the door from school one day and said, "I want to talk with you."

I had no idea of what this "talk" was going to be about and

asked whether I could at least change my clothes first—I had just finished playing field hockey with my high school team—but she persisted. I hesitantly sat down on the gray vinyl chair in the kitchen, just a few feet away from where she was sitting at the head of the table, smoking her Pall Mall cigarette. She had a stern look on her face and was staring straight at me with her angry brown eyes as if I had done something wrong. My heart was pounding with fear, and I just wanted to get this over with so I could get away from her glare.

After a moment, she blurted out, "I need to tell you that you were conceived before your dad and I married. Then, when I was in the hospital after you were born, I found out that your father went out with an old girlfriend. I was very upset and angry, and as a result I did not want your father to have anything to do with you. I am telling you this because I do not want you to make the same mistakes as I did."

I couldn't understand why she was telling me this information, and I hated her for it. Her decision to create distance between my father and me impacted our relationship throughout our entire lives. I saw her as weak and could not understand how she could think I would ever be like her; I had been unlike her throughout my whole childhood. She was talking to me as if I had done something wrong when *she* had made a mistake. I pushed my chair back away from the table, ran upstairs to my room, and slammed the door, shouting "I hate you! I hate you!"

In that moment, I lost respect for her and made a commitment to never be like her and to never have intercourse with any man before I was married. I also saw my father in a new light. I wondered if he truly loved my mother or if he felt trapped into doing the right thing and getting married after an accidental pregnancy. At sixteen I was not capable of asking him that question, and I now wish I'd had the courage to hear his side of the story rather than relying on my mother's viewpoint. I decided that when I had a daughter of my own, I would promote a wonderful relationship between her and her father, and this is a promise that I have been able to keep.

When I was in therapy years later, I came to understand that my mother was just trying to look out for me and prevent me from going down the same path that she had. However, it certainly didn't feel like it at the time.

While I enjoyed my social life in high school, my focus was on my academics. I didn't want to just get married and have kids, I wanted to pursue a meaningful career. We had ability groupings in our high school, and I had been placed in the "A" track, which was designated as the higher ability grouping. This meant that we received books that were more challenging to read than the "B" and "C" tracks. The teachers were always complimentary toward us and would tell us how they loved teaching our classes, and we were designated as the college-bound kids.

In contrast, Sonny was placed in a "special" class for "retarded" children due to his borderline IQ. Initially, I felt hurt and helpless. There were a lot of verbal assaults from the other kids at school once they heard about the situation, so I then became very defensive and later denied knowing him. I was ashamed to be his sister, and I did not want the other kids to know I had a brother in the "special" class. It was a difficult time for my relationship with my brother. We were only fifteen months apart in age, but we were a whole world apart in our personalities and school experiences.

When I was seventeen, I learned that my brother's teacher thought he should not have been placed in these classes. When I discovered this, I was upset with my parents for not questioning the school system about his initial testing and placement. They just accepted that this was where he belonged. I was so angry with them for allowing this to happen to him. They were his parents, and I felt they did not protect him from this sad stigma and school experience.

Years later, when I was in psychotherapy, I learned that Sonny was also affected by the chaos that occurred in our family. We each had our own reaction to the environment we grew up in, and Sonny's stresses showed up in his school work.

As I approached the end of my high school years, I had to decide what career path I wanted to take. The choices for women in the 1950s were to be a teacher, nurse, secretary, airline stewardess, or housewife. These jobs were not considered to be "men's work," so they were socially acceptable—careers such as being a doctor, lawyer, accountant, or airline pilot were strongly discouraged.

There was also an underlying societal expectation that women would only go to college to find a successful husband to take care of them. What you studied was not important because you would just get married and have a family and never use what you learned. This was often called getting your "Mrs." degree, and it was a mindset that prevailed all of the way into the mid to late 1980s. Men were expected to work and support their families while women were expected to stay home and take care of the children and home while also providing a social life for their family by keeping in touch with relatives and friends. In retrospect, this kind of underlying societal norm gave the message that women were not as valuable since men were responsible for being the financial stronghold of a family. Whatever job a woman may hold is secondary and not important. It should be of no surprise that many women experienced feelings of low self-esteem, especially if they were dependent on their husbands. We are, after all, a product of the society we are brought up in.

I never, ever agreed with this societal expectation. My dream was to be independent of my husband so I could choose the path I wanted in life without his permission. Some women at this time did choose to pursue a career, and it was considered to be acceptable as long as it was a choice and not a forced decision due to having an unemployed husband or being unable to get married.

My mother was not someone who wanted to pursue a career. She worked for a short time in a shoe factory in the late 1940s to help save money to buy their house in Massapequa Park. I know she did not like her job, and she often came home with migraine headaches after work. In the mid-1950s she went back to work as a maid in the hospital to help out with the family finances, and again she often came home with a migraine headache and would lie down in her bed for several hours after work. She was perfectly happy to stay at home and fill the traditional homemaker role, but I am not my mother, and this was not the life I wanted for myself.

After some thought, I decided that I wanted to go to nursing school. It was a profession I thought would be interesting and would provide a financial independence that I could rely on for the rest of my life. And, most importantly, the cost of schooling was affordable for me and my parents. However, when I shared this news with my mother, she immediately dismissed my dream by saying, "You think you are above us! Don't think you will ever attract a doctor, because once he discovers your background, he will never marry you." She then went on to tell me that it wasn't possible to send me to nursing school as they did not have the money for it, and that I should be happy working in a factory like she did. Through all of this, my father was passive and quiet.

I felt so horrible about myself after this conversation. In spite of my success in school and in my social life, I felt like a fraud and a phony. I was surrounded by friends who were college-bound and had no money issues to hold them back, and even though they accepted me for who I was, I was starting to feel as if I didn't belong. I threw books against the wall and slammed doors in my frustration with my mom's attitude. Not only was she completely unsupportive of my dream, but she had also implied that my only goal was to marry a doctor. She was once again projecting her own life experiences onto me and using them as an excuse to hold me back.

I hated my mother for this lack of support and encouragement and was determined that I wouldn't end up working in a factory like she did. I was capable of more than this, and I had to keep my belief that I could be more than she was.

# Chapter 5

## Like Mother, like Daughter

The rest of my high school years were full of after-school activities. I was involved in field hockey, volleyball, and the sports club in my junior and senior year, and I also sang in our high school choir and was a member of the Future Nurses of America and drama clubs. I was inducted into the Phi Beta Chi sorority in my sophomore year, and my friends during these years—Pat Mollo, Sandy Wange, Ellen McGarr, Carol Zider, Kathy Hanrahan, Jane Powell, and others—were important peer influences on me. We attended parties and raised money for the Red Cross in addition to having sleepovers with other friends.

I had another group of friends—Joyce Blockis, Lois Blank, Lois Leonard, Robert Calhoun, Jack Farley, and others—who loved spending their summers at Tobay Beach in Wantagh, New York. We would slather ourselves with baby oil and iodine to get as tan as we could—this was before we knew about the risk of getting skin cancer—and talk about what we were planning to do after high school, what colleges we wanted to apply to, and of course, boyfriends. As I listened to my friends, I tried to figure out what I was going to do now that I knew I didn't have my parents' support.

Pat and I thought about being airline stewardesses because it sounded like a glamorous job, and because the cost to pursue this career was very low compared to going to college. I decided to apply to the different airlines to see what my options were, and I was accepted by one of the major airlines between my junior and senior year of high school. However, the more I learned about this profession, the less appealing it sounded. In the 1950s, airline stewardesses dressed very formally, and there were no pants allowed. You were judged on your attractiveness, your weight, and your measurements. If you gained weight, you were fired. Once I heard that stewardesses had to light the cigars of businessmen and fix drinks, and that they were considered "a waitress in the sky," I decided I could no longer pursue this job.

Pat and I also looked into the nursing profession as another option, especially as we had both been members of the Future Nurses of America club. We shared all of our hopes and dreams, and she knew of my financial concerns and the dilemma I faced with my mother. She was a wonderful friend. She came from an Italian background and her parents were very supportive of her career aspirations, even though they didn't view college as being overly important. I spent a lot of time at her home since she was an only child and I enjoyed being around her mother and father.

At the end of the summer in 1959, just before I started my senior year of high school, my parents sat Sonny and me down and said they had something to tell us. We wondered what it could possibly be; they had never acted like this before. My mother excitedly said, "I know you both are wondering what this is about, so I'll get straight to it. We just want to tell you we are going to have another baby!"

I could hardly believe what I was hearing. "What!" I said. "Are you kidding me? You are both too old to have another baby!" My mother was thirty-eight years old, and my father was forty-one. This had come completely out of the blue; I hadn't even known that they wanted another kid. They did not seem surprised at our disbelief—I am sure they felt the same themselves.

They continued on to tell us that the baby was due at the end of May 1960. My father simply said, "We hope you both will be as happy as we feel."

I did *not* feel happy about them having a baby. I felt numb and angry. I was going to be graduating high school on June 26 of that year, and now I was going to have to share this special time with a new baby. I was so looking forward to finally having my accomplishments recognized by my family, and now their attention would be elsewhere. I also felt embarrassed because I did not know anyone else my age who was in this situation. Times have certainly changed and having kids later in life is much more common today, but this was unusual back then. Sonny was quiet throughout the whole exchange; the news did not seem to matter to him.

This situation reminded me of how my grandmother became pregnant at the exact same time as my mother became pregnant with me. I wondered if my mother felt as invisible at the news of her mother's pregnancy as I did now.

The news also hit me especially hard because I realized that in a few months my mother would have to leave her job as a cleaning woman at the Meadowbrook Hospital, which meant my parents definitely could not afford to help me with any tuition for nursing school, no matter how small that help may have been. If I wanted to continue my schooling, it was now completely up to me to come up with the money for tuition.

I spent my senior year trying to figure out what I wanted to do and how to get where I wanted to go. Then, the answer came when I learned that my friend Pat and another sorority sister Janet Inglis, were both applying to the Mount Vernon School of Nursing, which was located in the Bronxville area of New York. It was a three-year diploma school instead a four-year college program so the tuition was much lower, but the school was considered the best school to attend to become a "real" nurse. It primarily focused on the clinical aspects of nursing, as opposed to the college program which had an emphasis on academics and often lead to teaching classes to nursing students.

I applied to several diploma programs and went through the interview process with Pat and Janet. We were all accepted to the Mount Vernon School of Nursing in the spring of 1960, along with another classmate Holly Geiger. To ensure that I could get enough money to pay for my first year of tuition, I applied to several hospitals to work as a nurse aide over the summer and was accepted at Mercy Hospital in Rockville Center. I would make four hundred dollars, which was just enough to cover my tuition and expenses for the next year. I was ecstatic. I could hardly believe that I was actually going to be a nurse! I once again had a sense of belonging with my peers because I was moving forward with my life, just like they were, and we could celebrate our future success together.

This wonderful and happy news was soon eclipsed when I found out that my brother was eligible to graduate high school at the same time as I was. I was unduly upset that yet another injustice had been done to me. How could Sonny, who was fifteen months younger than me and in a "special" class for slow children, now be graduating with my class? In looking back, I can only assume that my brother had fewer requirements to graduate than I did. At the time, though, all I knew was that my moment was being overshadowed by yet another sibling.

In retrospect, I was an angry teenager who was lashing out at the people around me. However, this was a difficult time for me. There was no acknowledgment of my success from my parents, and I felt so invisible. I had seen my graduation as one of the few opportunities to receive acknowledgment from my family, and now I would be sharing this moment with my younger brother and a new baby. I fought an inner battle to take the high road and be happy for Sonny. It was not an easy task.

On May 26, 1960, Guy Robert was born. Despite my initial reaction to his impending arrival, I loved Guy. He did not ask to be born, and this situation was not his fault. He was so adorable with his dark brown hair and brown eyes, and I came to love him more than I could have imagined.

I went through the motions at my high school graduation with Sonny and celebrated the arrival of my new brother at a ceremony at our home with our close family members. Our relatives congratulated us, and they were very interested in hearing about the nursing school that I would be attending in the fall. This was validating for me, but this feeling would vanish as their attention would quickly shift to my brothers.

Soon after I graduated, I started my first job as a nurse aide. I was assigned to work on the maternity ward, which was a wonderful place to start because all of the new mothers were healthy and excited to meet their babies. I loved the feeling of receiving my first paycheck, and all of the money went into saving for my next year's tuition.

While working as a nurse aide gave me valuable experience,

it also taught me that I would not want to stay in this position for very long. The hospital I worked at was a Catholic hospital that was run by nuns, and the sisters were not very easy to work for. They were serious most of the time, and they often barked their orders at me. On one occasion, someone had spilled some water and I was told in a harsh tone to get on the floor and wipe it up! I felt so humiliated. I became even more determined to become a nurse and be in a position of authority, and I decided that once I was in this position, I would treat the people around me with respect.

Finally, the day arrived when I would move to the Mount Vernon School of Nursing. All of the students were required to live on the premises in a dormitory located across the street from the hospital for the duration of the three-year program. In the summer you worked in the hospital as a nurse as part of the internship, which is why the tuition was so much lower than the college programs.

My friends and I were all incredibly excited to be a part of the nursing program. We had bought new bedding and brought comfort pillows and family photos from home to decorate our rooms. They placed Pat, Holly, and me in a very large three-bedroom suite that was formerly assigned to the director of nursing, while Janet was placed in a single room. Pat and I did almost everything together, and at first it was fun. However, I soon began to realize how difficult it was to study with roommates around, especially because there were a lot of people visiting our room each evening. I remember wishing that I had my own space, and I envied Janet for having her own room and being independent of any friend alliances.

The rest of the girls in our class of fifty students were very different from the people I had known in high school. Most of them had gone to an all-girl school and were now free for the first time in their lives—I guess that was true of all of us, but it was even more evident in this group. I remember that most of them started to drink and stayed out late, and they were a bit wild. I felt out of place around these women.

When we first entered the school, I loved the idea of becoming a student nurse and wearing a uniform. After six months we would receive our white head caps and a navy-blue cape in a special ceremony, signifying that we had passed our trial as a student nurse. However, I quickly learned that the program was not what I expected.

Our first week in the program included an introduction by Ms. McGann, one of our first-year nursing instructors. With a stern voice, she said, "Welcome, students, to the Mount Vernon School of Nursing. I want to share with you the protocol for what will be expected of you during the next three years. First of all, your dorm is just across the street from the hospital, and you are all to be in bed by 10:00 PM. You will have all of your meals in the hospital cafeteria, and we do not allow any fraternizing between you and the Dominican Republic interns and resident doctors. In addition, when you all receive your blue and white striped uniforms in four weeks, you will have a perfectly starched white apron, white stockings, and white shoes. Your uniform must be below the knee. Your hair must be no longer than shoulder length. If your hair is long, you must wear a hair net that does not reach the collar of your uniform. You will be inspected every morning before leaving the nurses residence to ensure you are all in compliance."

While this speech was a little intimidating, my friends and I got the sense that we were about to enter a challenging course of study and felt proud to be a part of this profession. However, we would soon learn that these expectations were not to be taken lightly.

We were watched constantly by our instructors. Ms. McGann was a real bitch; she could be so cutting and would make snide remarks about some little thing you did. For example, when we were learning to make a bed with square corners, if you did not get it exactly right she would come over, pull the sheet out, and make you do it again in front of the class. The anxiety I felt around getting on her bad side made me feel ill.

We had an older woman who was our house mother at our student dorm. Once 10:00 PM passed, she would come by each room with her flashlight and shine it under our doorway to make sure we were all in bed.

The expectation that really got to me was that when we were working on the floors of the hospital and had to chart what we did with our patients, we were expected to get up off our chairs when the always-male doctor came in so he could do his own chart. We could only continue our own work when they were finished. I cannot tell you how demeaning this felt to me.

I did not think of myself as rebellious when I was in high school—other than the attitude and frustration I felt around the lack of support from my parents—but I certainly rebelled against this program. I missed home and my baby brother, Guy. Pat and I would go home most weekends, making the long drives back and forth to spend a total of three hours with our parents. This put stress on our already-full schedule, leaving us with not much time to study.

Six months after we entered the program, Pat and I decided to leave. Neither of us were happy there. Pat had decided she did not want to be a nurse at all; I still wanted to be a nurse, but I was having a hard time adjusting to the seemingly nonsensical strictness of the program. Depressed and exhausted, I called my father and told him I wanted to leave. He asked if I was sure, if I could hang in a little longer before making this decision, but I just begged to come home. I left the program in February 1961 and found a job as a ward clerk on the pediatric unit of a hospital near my parents' house a month later. It was hard to return home, but outside of my brother Guy, nothing else mattered to me.

My mother continued to try to protect me from the world in the worst way. There was one evening when my new friend Laurie Kalinowski and I went to an intern and resident party. My mom kept calling until she finally got hold of someone, who then came up to me to say I had to go home. This was another example of having something very innocent and fun turned into something ugly because she thought I was like her. She would have had sex with someone at the party, just like she did with my father, and she was projecting her reality onto these innocent circumstances. I became more aware of how different I was from her, and I hated her even more.

During this time off school, I lost almost twenty pounds—a symbolic measure of myself and my self-esteem. My weight had always been a measuring mark for me because my mother had been overweight and I did not want to look like her. However, even though I had been desperate to leave the nursing program, I felt disappointed and angry with myself for not finishing school. I felt confident in myself and in my belief that I could be and deserved to be a nurse, but at times I felt like a nobody because I did not complete my degree. I had saved up enough money for a year's tuition, so I made the decision to return to the Mount Vernon School of Nursing and complete my schooling. My friends Janet and Holly were still in the program, and I knew we could support each other.

I re-applied to go back to Mount Vernon School of Nursing

in the early spring of 1961, and they accepted my application. I felt a renewed determination to become a nurse and achieve my dreams, and I was determined that nothing was going to stop me.

My mother and father with Guy, a baby brother is born
May, 1960

# Chapter 6

### The First Date

In mid-August 1961, I decided to go out with my friends to the Ratskeller in Rockville Center, New York. It was one of the last weekends of the summer, and I was excited that I was going to return to school at the end of the month. I was nineteen years old and feeling very confident about myself on this balmy summer evening.

The Ratskeller was known as a fun college hangout. It was located down a cobblestone stairway that lead you to a dimly lit room with a bar. It was filled with young college kids, and there was lots of energy and talking going on all around us. The atmosphere was electrifying. After enjoying some small talk with a few people, I noticed that I was standing in a corner with a good-looking guy. He stood six feet, one inch tall with dark black hair, olive skin, and warm brown eyes, and I found myself to be attracted to him. I said hello to catch his attention and asked his name. It was loud in the room, so he smiled, positioned himself in front of me, placed his hand against the wall I was leaning on, and leaned his head forward to introduce himself as Ed Phelan. We talked for a while about our summers, and he had a fun sense of humor that made me laugh. I wished we met earlier in the evening; it was getting late, and I had to leave soon as I had to be up early the next day for work.

As I started to make my move to leave, he stopped me and asked, "Would you like to attend a wedding with me next weekend? One of my best friends is getting married in Queens, and I would like you to go with me. I will be in the wedding party, though, so I will have to arrange for someone to pick you up. Is that okay?"

I was interested but a bit apprehensive because of the distance—Queens is a good hour's drive from Massapequa Park. I had never been on a date that far away from home. Could I really trust him? I was suspicious of his intentions, but I also liked what I knew of him from our brief half-hour conversation. I told him that I would have to think about this invitation. He was very understanding, and we exchanged telephone numbers so I could tell him what my decision was.

Ed called me the next day and told me that his brother, Jerry, would be able to come and pick me up. He further explained that his mother and sister would be at the wedding, and that I could sit with them. It did sound like a fun event, and despite my initial skepticism I did feel that I could trust him. My decision was made. I was excited to know more about Ed, and about the rest of his family.

The day of the wedding arrived, and I decided to wear a straight black dress and black heels. Jerry came to the house and introduced himself, and I found him to be as handsome as Ed. I was so happy I decided to take the chance and go on this adventure of a date; this was definitely going to be a fun evening.

On the hour-long drive to Queens, Jerry told me all about

their family. He was twenty-one years old and Ed was twenty-three. They had a sister, Kathleen, who was seventeen. They had lost their father when the boys were eleven and thirteen years old, and they were very close with their mother.

I learned that Ed had graduated from St. John's University in New York and worked in the group insurance business, and that he was considering going to law school in the near future. Jerry had finished two years of college and was working in the sheet metal business as an apprentice. He loved the work he was doing and wanted to eventually run a company of his own. Their mother, Elsie, worked full time as a secretary and paid for her three children to attend college; I immediately respected who she was as a woman and mother.

Jerry also told me about the couple getting married, Jim and Pat. They were very good friends of Ed and had been together for two years. They were the first of their friends to get married.

As Jerry talked, I noticed his hazel eyes, freckles, and light brown hair, which complemented his six foot, two inch frame. It was interesting to me that I was going to be spending more time with Jerry than I did with Ed on this first date.

Jerry asked about my life, and I told him that this date was the boldest and most daring thing I had ever done and that it took a lot of courage for me to go through with it. I also told him that I was returning to Mount Vernon School of Nursing in a couple of weeks.

We finally arrived at the reception to find room bustling with the activity of one hundred and fifty guests and wedding party attendants. I looked for Ed and wondered how I was going to feel seeing him in this setting as opposed to the college bar scene. Trying to hide my nervousness about being surrounded by strangers in a strange city, I took a deep breath and smiled at the other guests while I searched for my assigned table.

Within minutes, I heard Ed's voice calling my name. He came over to me and proclaimed, "I am so happy you are here!" He then proceeded to take my hand and bring me across the dance floor to meet the bride and groom as well as the other members of the party. It was a hectic moment full of fun and laughter. He then walked me back to my table and introduced me to Elsie and Kathleen before returning to the dais where the wedding party was seated.

The dinner was pleasant, and I spent my time getting to know these two women. Elsie was a pleasant, reserved woman about five feet, four inches tall with brown eyes, gray highlights in her brown hair, and a medium build. Kathleen looked like her mother with shoulder-length brown hair and hazel eyes and was about five feet, six inches in height. She had a raspy voice and laughed very easily. She was a senior in high school and planned to attend college the following year so she could become a teacher.

After the dinner ended, the band began to play and everyone got up to dance. This was an Irish wedding with lots of Irish music, and the party was full of jokes and dancing. Ed and I danced to several songs, and I discovered he was pretty good at it. As I walked back to the table, Ed and his friends began gesturing at me and singing along with the band, "Here she is, Miss America." The evening was magical—it turned out to be one of the most fun nights in my life.

I saw Ed again the following weekend. We went out with his friends, and I enjoyed them as much as I had at the wedding. Unfortunately, I returned to school soon after and our time together became limited. Ed called me frequently so we could stay in touch, and we made plans to see one another about once a month.

I felt very confident upon returning to the nursing program

and was met with a lot of support from the director of nursing and my former nursing instructor Ms. McGann. I had thought that she did not like me during my first semester in the nursing program because she was intimidating and very critical in her responses to any questions. However, she was very supportive after I had left the school and had been instrumental in getting me back into the program. I was voted class president upon my return, and I became very engaged in my nursing and science classes.

Around this time, I began going to go to church every day. I had always been very religious, and I loved the rituals of the church; they gave me a sense of emotional support and comfort. My father was Catholic, and my mother had been Catholic as a child but had changed her religion to follow the Methodist Church by the time she met my father. My parents decided my brother and I would grow up in the Episcopal Church as a compromise, but now that I was older and surrounded by peers who were Catholic—including Ed—I found myself believing more in the philosophy of the Catholic Church and made the decision to convert. I started meeting with the priest every week in preparation, and Ed occasionally came to see the priest with me. My parents had no voice in my decision, and even if they did, they were too busy with my almost one-year-old baby brother to spend any energy fighting me.

Not long after I returned to school, Ed and I decided that we would exclusively date one another. I did not care to date anyone else, nor did I have the time. This was a very happy time for me; I loved being with Ed, and I was doing well in my studies.

When my two-week Christmas break arrived, I was looking forward to being home and seeing Ed on a more frequent basis. As we drove to Massapequa Park, we talked about his work and I shared my student nursing experiences. Then, when we reached the front of my house, he stopped the car and said he wanted to talk. He looked at me and said, "I love you, and I want to marry you."

I was not totally surprised by this statement—we had grown very close in the past few months—but it did catch me off guard and presented a problem. The nursing school had a policy that none of their students could be married during their time in the program. Since I was just nineteen years old I thought that we could sustain our relationship until I graduated, and I told him as much.

Ed responded that he was ready to get married, and he did not want to wait three years to do so. He then gave me an ultimatum: it was either him or school. I couldn't have both.

I was upset by this response. As much as I loved Ed, it was my dream to become a nurse. I said, "I just returned back to school five months ago, and I am class president and ranked highest in my class. I really want to be a nurse. I need to be independent and have a career to fall back on in my life, and I do not want to end up working in factory work or as a cleaning woman like my mother did. Give me time to think about this over the holidays before I make any decision." Without another word, we headed inside.

I felt so conflicted by this dilemma. I knew I wanted to be somebody with a professional degree, but I also knew that three years was a long time to wait for someone who was ready to be married, and I was afraid he would just find someone else that he would not have to wait for. I also didn't know how I was going to pay for the next two years of my schooling as my savings only covered the first year. I tried to let this decision go and enjoy my time with my family, but it kept intruding my thoughts. What would everyone think and say about me leaving nursing a second time? I knew that Ed's family valued education, and it was a big deal when Ed became the first college graduate in his family. What would they think of me if I let this dream go?

I realize now how alone I was at this time in my life. I did not talk about this decision with anyone, just like I had not discussed my plans to return to school. It was as if I had no parents, because they had no say in my life and decisions. I had seen the parents of my high school peers being very involved in my friends' decisions since they were paying for their education, but I did not have that same support. I had friends from high school that I kept in contact with, but I was also a very private person and did not share my thoughts or plans. The concern I felt around how I was going to pay for my next two years of schooling was unknown to anyone; I carried this burden alone.

It was because of this inner conflict and concern that I made the decision to leave school again and get married. This decision provided me with a way out of my financial dilemma and allowed me to be with the man that I loved. Getting engaged at almost twenty years of age was socially acceptable at the time, so I knew that I was unlikely to experience any resistance to this idea from the world around me. I was relieved to have finally decided what I was going to do, although I was disappointed with myself for once again leaving school.

On the Sunday after Christmas, I sat down with my parents in the living room and told them I was leaving school, and that Ed and I were to be engaged. My father asked if I was sure this is what I wanted, and I explained how I could not be married and go to school at the same time, and that Ed was not willing to wait. My father listened and was supportive of my decision, but I think he was concerned that I might once again be sorry that I left school.

My mother did not say anything as she was busy being a mother to my baby brother, but I think that she was pleased with my decision. She never supported me going to school. She liked Ed and was most likely happy that I would be taken care of by him.

In looking back, it is interesting that despite all my aspirations, I chose to leave school and marry a man who had the same attitude as my mother. I once took a class on family therapy and learned that when we get married, we unconsciously choose a partner who is at the same level of pathology as we are in order to work out our own family issues. Sadly, I was fighting against my mother's attitude in my relationship with Ed, as well as against all of the societal norms of the 1950s. It is no wonder I spent most of my adult life in therapy trying to overcome these attitudes.

I told Ed about my decision, and then we went to his home to tell his family the news. We walked into the living room and Elsie, Jerry, and Kathleen were all sitting together. Ed excitedly said, "We have something to tell you. Lilly and I are going to get engaged, and she decided to leave nursing school so we can be married."

The reaction here was quite different, although not unexpected. At first, there was an uncomfortable silence. I knew they thought I should have stayed in school because education was very important to Elsie. Eventually, though, they all got up and gave us a hug, saying they were happy they for us but were also surprised. I felt their disapproval in my choice, and the look on their faces remains embedded in my mind. The decision had been made, though, and I now had to live with the consequences.

Later that night, once we were alone, Ed turned to me and said, "Okay, now that you made your decision, I do not want

you to come back later and say you want to go back to school."
I heard him, but I knew it was a promise that I couldn't make.
I needed to complete myself as a person, and I would just have
figure something out in the future. Someday, somehow, I was
going to be a nurse.

# Chapter 7

## The Marriage

Ed and I officially became engaged in the spring of 1961 and eventually set a date for May 11, 1963. In retrospect, I can see that I could have almost finished nursing school by the time we actually got married. However, I decided there was no point in looking back at what could have been and instead focused on looking forward to a new life together with Ed.

Having left nursing school, I was now back home living with my parents as well as Sonny, who was nineteen years old, and Guy, who was one and a half. My parents were happy that I was marrying Ed, but I did not care what they thought. I had been supporting myself for long enough that I felt they no longer had any influence on my decisions. I found a job at the telephone company in Hempstead, New York and began working on the vision of my perfect wedding.

Ed and I spent a lot of time on the weekends with his friends in Flushing, New York, including Jim and Pat from the wedding. Jim was a teacher and Pat was working as a secretary at the time we met. She also wanted to be a nurse but had put off her own career ambitions when she decided to marry Jim. At this point she was pregnant with their first child, and this was an exciting time for them. Ed and I had never discussed the possibility of children; the idea seemed foreign and unreal to me.

Another couple we hung out with was Linda and Joe. Linda was a college graduate who taught middle school and Joe was completing his law studies at night and working during the day. There was also Sonny, Ed's best friend who had recently graduated college, and his girlfriend Ginger, who did not go to college and was working as a secretary. We spent time with Jerry, Ed's brother, and his girlfriend Pat, whom he had met a few months after I met Ed. She was a nurse working in public health. Most of the group were three to four years older than I and we all got along very well, at least on the surface.

I had always been considered attractive, and now that I had left nursing school I focused on my appearance as a way to feel good about myself. I worked on keeping my weight down and bought nice clothes to keep up on the latest fashions. However, whenever I was around Pat I would feel inferior since she was a nurse, but I was not. She embodied who I wanted to be as a woman. Pat and Linda were both very social and outgoing, and I was quiet in their presence. I did my best to act as if I was an equal to them, but I did not feel that way about myself. I cried a lot, both by myself and with Ed whenever I felt he did not love me—a symptom of the fact that I did not love myself. Thankfully, Ed was very patient and understanding of my moods.

My sense of inferiority was very hard to deal with when I was around my future in-laws. Pat lived nearby in Queens, New York and spent a lot of time at the Phelan home, having dinners with the family during the week and becoming close to Kathleen and Elsie. In contrast, I lived a good hour away and only saw the family on the occasional weekend. I felt very much outside of the family circle. I wished I had my nursing degree; then, I would not feel so alone.

I was no longer a self-assured, confident person, and the pain of not belonging left me feeling like a boat without its rudder. I felt invisible around these strong female personalities, and at times felt I wanted to die. I overcame these emotions by holding on to the thought that I would become a nurse in time, and I overcompensated for my perceived lack of worth by keeping my weight down, dressing well, and planning an elegant wedding.

One day, several months after we became engaged, Ed called to chat. During our conversation, he said, "I was talking to my aunt Kate and she said you are so quiet that she felt that you would affect my business career." I felt sick to my stomach. Finally, I managed to ask, "What made her say this to you?" He dismissively responded, "It does not matter what she thinks." It definitely mattered to me.

After this conversation, I would hear these words over and over each time I saw his aunt, whom he was very close to and had a significant role in the family. I will never forget the pain and hurt I felt after hearing this during such a vulnerable time in my life. This only confirmed my feelings of being lesser than the rest of his family and friends. I would often ask myself, why did he tell me this? Did he want to call off the engagement? I never asked him, though, and he never again brought up this conversation.

Ed bought me a beautiful diamond ring for our engagement celebration. It was a carat and a quarter in size, with a brilliant color and a slight flaw which could not be seen by the naked eye. It was beautiful. We had a fun and happy engagement party in my parents' backyard with all of our favorite family and friends.

I loved my engagement ring, but I always felt self-conscious about the flaw and wondered whether it was symbolic of our relationship. Ed and I had decided the flaw was not a problem because of the diamond's shiny brilliance, but in retrospect the ring was a mirror image of my relationship with Ed. On the surface we were a young, good-looking couple with the promise of a wonderful future together. The flaw in the diamond was me, not fully developed enough as a woman to make this marriage bright and successful.

As the wedding approached, we attended the mandatory prenuptial classes at the Catholic church. We went to weekly meetings with the priest to go over what was required to make a marriage in the eyes of God. At one point, the priest jokingly said to me in front of Ed, "Are you sure you don't want to be a nun?" I laughed this off, but perhaps he saw something in me that I was not able to see myself.

After the last session, the priest took me aside and said, "Are you sure you want to go ahead with this marriage?" I answered, "Of course I do. Why do you ask?" He said he just wanted to be sure, but I found this exchange a bit disconcerting,

It is also interesting that my wedding bouquet was made in the form of a rosary bead. I had white roses with opaque beads in between them and a silver cross at the bottom. It was symbolic of where I was at this time in my life; church was my refuge, and I was feeling very religious. Perhaps this feeling was what the priest had picked up on in his discussions with me.

Our wedding finally arrived, and we had a beautiful day at The Huntington Town House in Long Island, New York. We had four bridesmaids and four groomsmen. Jerry was Ed's best man and Pat, my best friend from high school, was my maid of honor. As I was getting ready to walk down the aisle with my father, the priest again came over to me and said, "You know, it is not too late to change your mind. Are you sure you want to do this?"

I thought he must be testing me, so I just said quietly, "Yes, I am sure."

The wedding march began, and I looked at my handsome father in his black tuxedo and saw his soft blue eyes moisten. As I walked with him down the aisle, I trembled and sobbed all the way. Luckily, the thick veil over my face hid my tears.

The wedding ceremony was performed, and Ed and I became husband and wife. We held hands as we walked together to the back of the church and were greeted by all of our guests throwing rice into the air. It was an emotional experience for me, although the priest questioning my marriage still nagged at the back of my mind. I have thought back to this conversation many times since then, and I still am not sure what he sensed about me or Ed.

The Huntington Town House was supposed to be one of the best places to have a wedding reception. It was surrounded by large trees, and the entrance off the circular driveway opened to a large foyer with several banquet rooms. There was a light, airy feel to the foyer, and the energy surrounding the room was invigorating. Photos were being taken by a professional photographer and our family and friends were chattering away while drinking champagne and soft drinks and eating hors d'oeuvres. It could not have been a more perfect day. There was a lot of dancing and laughter, and of course there were the usual jokes from the guys about joining the world of marriage.

After the afternoon reception, Ed and I stopped by my paternal grandmother's home. She was fragile at the time and could not see very well, and I wanted her to see me in my wedding dress and give her my bouquet. As I entered the kitchen where she was sitting in her usual spot by the window, she looked up at me with the biggest smile I can ever remember. My heart swelled with love as I presented her with the flowers and cross. It was a special moment between us.

When my grandmother passed away in November 1964, the rosary was missing. I knew that her wicked sister lived with her at the time, and after having upended the house looking for it, I am convinced that her sister stole it. I have learned to let it go, but I was disappointed that I could not have it buried with her.

The next stop for Ed and me was the Phelan house for an afterparty gathering with his family and friends. We had changed our clothes at my grandmother's home so we could just relax and continue to party until around midnight before heading off to check in to the hotel at the La Guardia Airport. When we first entered the hotel room, we noticed there was a crib set up and I wondered if it was a sign of something to come. Ed and I laughed about it and then crashed, since we had an early flight to Bermuda the next morning for our honeymoon.

I had never been on a plane before, and though I was excited about the trip I hadn't thought about it much between my work and the wedding plans. Once we were in the air, I could relax and enjoy looking out the airplane window at the beautiful blue-green water surrounding Bermuda. Unfortunately, the end of the flight was not as pleasant. I started feeling a bit queasy as we descended, but I kept taking deep breaths to calm myself. Then, just before landing, I became physically ill and had to use the bag in front of my seat! I felt so embarrassed.

We arrived at a beautiful hotel located right on the water and were escorted to a room with an ocean view. We were given the itinerary with the dinner schedule and the many activities we could enjoy during our week on the island. We were looking forward to touring the island on motor scooters, but that would have to wait a few days so I could get over the air sickness and recover from the aftermath of the wedding.

The next morning, I rolled over and drowsily looked out the hotel window at the Atlantic Ocean off the Bermuda coast. "Good morning Mrs. Phelan," I heard my new husband say.

I sat up, looked over at Ed lying in the bed next to me, and hesitantly smiled. "Good morning, Mr. Edward Phelan."

My name, my life, everything was as new and as unfamiliar as this exotic honeymoon. We spent our trip easing ourselves into married life and enjoying each other's company. During the day, we explored the island on our motor scooters and ate out at different restaurants. Every night we went out and listened to the bongo drums and danced the night away. As we strolled down the beach, hand in hand, we looked like the perfect honeymoon couple. The trip was wonderful.

However, my apprehension about sex was a constant undercurrent to everything we did. I had never been alone with Ed until the night at the hotel by the airport, and up until that point I had never thought about the first time I would be intimate with someone. I never talked about sex with my friends or mother, but I thought that it would be natural, and that I would be okay with it once we were married. Now that I was on my honeymoon and I knew my husband was going to expect us to have an intimate evening, I became anxious and afraid. After a lifetime of believing that it wasn't okay to have sex, I was having a hard time feeling as if it was okay now.

Throughout the first day of our trip, I found myself getting more and more nervous about what the evening would hold. After dinner, I suggested going out for a walk instead of going back to our room, claiming to be uncomfortable. As we walked along the ocean with the balmy breeze blowing around us, I realized I was avoiding having sex with Ed. All these years I had been determined that I was never going to be like my mother. I told myself that I would never have intercourse before getting married, no matter how tempting it might be, because I didn't want to have a child out of wedlock. All of these defenses that I had built up for years didn't just disappear when I said, "I do."

Despite my hesitation, I knew it was probably time to make love now that I was married, and after our walk we made our way upstairs to our room. It was time. I was given a white sheer night gown and a matching cover at my wedding shower, and I put it on and walked over to the bed where Ed was waiting for me. He was very loving and gentle with me. We kissed and held one another, touching and feeling each other like we had done before, but this time we didn't stop there. This was the night I was going to lose my virginity.

When we finally consummated the marriage, it was not what I expected. I was in pain and did not want to do it again. Being a virgin was so ingrained in my psyche that I could not allow myself to suddenly enjoy this act. In retrospect, I was ill prepared for marriage. The rest of the week I did everything possible to avoid repeating this pain. Ed had no sense of what was going on with me internally as I had long ago learned how to hide my true feelings, but he was very accepting of my discomfort around having sex and was very patient with me at this vulnerable time.

By the end of our week-long honeymoon, I had gained seven pounds. I had always been conscious about my weight and would eat a restricted diet at home as it was one of the few ways that I could enact some control over my life. Here in

Bermuda, though, my anxiety about having sex was high, and I turned to the delicious food for comfort.

Our honeymoon was a fun and emotional time for me, and I was looking forward to going home to start our new life together. Little did I know how unprepared I was for the reality of married life.

My wedding party on May 11th 1963

Lilly and Ed Phelan's wedding on May 11th 1963 with Lillian and
Stanley Radziewicz

# Chapter 8

## Our New Home

When our wedding was still approaching, Ed and I had decided to rent the top floor of a two-story house that was located on a beautiful tree-lined street in an established neighborhood in Queens, New York. The homes were located on a hilltop, so there were two flights of brick-lined stairs that led to the main entrance of the home and another flight after that to get to our fully-furnished apartment.

We moved in the day that we returned from our honeymoon. After entering our new home, we put down our suitcases, held each other's hand, and took a look around. To the left of the main entrance was our large bedroom with two twin beds pushed together, a dresser, and two end tables. The room was decorated with a floral wallpaper that seemed to be more suited to an older couple, but we embraced it with our love and our new life together.

To the right of the entrance was a small room with a sofa, a TV table, an arm chair, and a similar floral wallpaper in the bedroom. It looked very warm and cozy. Next we found the kitchen, which was a good size and had a Formica table and chairs with gray vinyl cushions. The sink was similar to the one my paternal grandmother had in her house—a white porcelain double sink with white cabinets underneath—and there was a gas stove next to it.

I remember looking out of our new kitchen window that first day and feeling overwhelmed. There were so many changes going on in my life. Outside of the six months I spent living in a nursing dormitory, this was the first time that either of us had lived with anyone outside of our parents' home. I loved Ed and he loved me, but we were both unprepared about what marriage meant on a day-to-day basis. I had never cooked before in my life—outside of the miraculous cream puffs my friend Sharon Agnone and I had made when we were ten years old—and I was now expected to cook for Ed and myself every day. I never thought to discuss cooking with any of my friends, assuming I would automatically know what to do. I had also quit my job at the telephone company before we left on our honeymoon because I knew we would be moving to a new area, so I didn't even have the familiarity of work to fall back on. I had no idea to how to start my new life as Mrs. Edward Phelan. Why didn't anyone tell me about this part of being married?

I was determined to be the perfect wife for Ed, but I struggled to think of what to make for our first few dinners in our new home. I had this notion that I needed to make a three-course meal every night, with a salad and dessert as well as a main course. I made meatloaf dinners, steak, spaghetti and meatballs, and ham with all the vegetables and bread and butter that I had deemed to be necessary after glancing through the magazines in the supermarket check-out stand. Despite being someone who always worked hard to maintain the optimal weight, food was still my outlet for my stress. I gained another ten pounds over the next two months, and Ed gained weight as well.

Once we got settled in to our new home, Ed returned to work at the Guardian Life Insurance Company while I stayed home. After two weeks of this, I decided to return to work because I wanted to feel useful. I found a job as a dental assistant for an oral surgeon who had a practice near where we lived, and after interviewing for the position I was immediately offered the job. I was nervous when I approached Ed about taking the job as I wasn't sure how he would feel about me going back to work, but thankfully he told me that it sounded great and he thought I would like it. I was so relieved; a job would be something for me, something I could be proud of doing.

I finally felt as if my life was getting back on track, except for one small thing: my period was late. My cycle was due to start eight days after our wedding and usually ran like clockwork, but now it was three weeks later and there was still no period. At first I thought it was caused by all of the changes in my life. I didn't think it was possible for me to be pregnant because Ed and I hardly had sex because of my discomfort, and when we were intimate we used the rhythm method of birth control. Once I was going on a month past due, though, I made an appointment with a gynecologist that my friend Pat had recommended.

A few weeks later I found myself sitting in the gynecologist's office. I had a magazine on my lap but was too nervous to concentrate on even flipping through the pages. At age twenty-one, I had never had a pelvic exam before, and I was apprehensive about what was to come. Finally, after what felt like an eternity, the nurse called my name and led me into the office.

The doctor was a very nice and handsome man with dark

hair and warm blue eyes. I was relieved when he had me sit in a comfortable arm chair across from him in a wood-paneled room so he could talk to me before the exam.

He asked, "What are you feeling? Do you have a tenderness in your breasts? Nausea? Weight gain?"

"Oh, yes," I replied. "Especially nausea. When I first wake up in the morning, I have to throw up immediately. After that, I am fine the rest of the day."

He wrote down my answers before continuing. "I see you are newly married. How is this going for you?"

I did not know how to answer this question as I had no frame of reference to judge how good or bad my marriage, so I remained silent. I hadn't known what to expect in this meeting, and I was starting to feel as if I was under a microscope.

He asked a few more questions and I answered them as best I could, and I felt a bit more at ease as time went on. He finally examined me and took a urine test, and a few minutes later he came back with the news.

"Yes, young lady, you are pregnant."

I was in shock. I felt like my body had betrayed me—I didn't *want* to be pregnant. How could this possibly be happening?

The doctor proceeded to explain, "You need to watch your weight, since you have gained seventeen pounds in the two months that you have been married. I want to see you every month for the next nine months, and I want you to write down everything you eat and drink. If you have any questions, you can always call me."

I left the office overwhelmed and in disbelief. There were so many changes happening in my life, and I wasn't sure how to feel about this one. When I got home, I took some time to just absorb this information and to try to come to terms with this reality.

After dinner that evening, I decided it was time to tell Ed. I wasn't sure how he was going to react to the news; we still really hadn't discussed children at all. After clearing the dinner plates, I took a moment to calm my nerves and then sat back down at the table. "Ed," I started, trying to keep my nervousness out of my voice, "I'm pregnant." Silence. Ed stared at me, and I couldn't read his expression. *Oh no*, I thought, *he really doesn't want to be a father.*

After a few tense moments, Ed broke out into a grin and asked, "Really?" He was so happy, although he was also in disbelief. We talked for a while longer about the baby, making plans and suggesting names, and I was relieved to see Ed so excited.

Telling our family and friends became the event of the year, besides our wedding of course, and everyone was very happy for us. My mother was happy to become a grandparent, and so was my father. Ed could not stop telling everyone he met. I was happy as well, but I was not quite as excited as he was. It wasn't his body that being flooded with all these hormones and life changes.

My new job started the week after I got the news, and I was happy to be back working in a medical setting. I was being trained to assist the dentist, an oral surgeon, in extracting diseased teeth. However, I was already starting to get tired a lot, and as the pregnancy progressed it became more and more difficult to work. I would wake up nauseous every morning and started to get headaches as well. I felt sick to my stomach when I heard and saw the dentist crack a tooth as it was being extracted. I noticed a sign in the x-ray room, which I frequently needed to enter to obtain the dental x-rays, warning about the hazards for pregnant women, and I worried about the effects it would have on the baby.

I was so overwhelmed and confused about to what to do in this situation. I wondered if I should just tell my new employer I was pregnant so I could avoid anything that was potentially harmful, or if I was being oversensitive. Unfortunately, there was no other position available in this small office, so I couldn't just switch out to a safer job. I was not sure how Ed and his family would view me if I left this new job prematurely, but it seemed to me that I was putting my baby at risk in the x-ray room. I decided I was going to resign, and Ed agreed.

Now that I was without work, I started to think about nursing school again. I looked into Nassau Community College in Garden City, New York, since my cousin Walter was also a nursing student there. They had a two-year part-time program to get an associate degree in nursing, and the more I thought about it the more I wanted to do it. I needed to do something more with my life than just being a homemaker.

I knew that Ed would not like to hear about me going back to school; he had made that clear when we first got engaged. However, I needed to listen to the strong voice within me that was not going away. I was alone within myself and needed to feel the fear of Ed's disapproval and declare my intentions anyway.

Sure enough, when I told Ed about my plan, he was less than pleased. He said, "You know, I told you when we decided to get engaged that I did not want you to mention this issue again!"

I stood firm. "Yes, I know, and I thought my desire to be a nurse would go away. But ever since I left school, I have felt worse and worse about myself. I am telling you, I will be a better wife and mother if I can become the woman I want to be."

Ed argued a bit more, but eventually he backed down and

reluctantly agreed that I could return to school—I think the fact that I was pregnant with our child helped him to come to terms with this short-term goal of going to school for the fall semester. The baby was due in February 1964, so I was already planning on taking the spring semester off so I could spend time with my baby before continuing my classes again in the summer. This may have seemed like less of a commitment to Ed, which may have helped him be more open to the idea.

And just like that, I was once again on the path to becoming a nurse, like I had always wanted to be.

# Chapter 9

## Back in School

I began school in the fall semester of 1963 by taking English 101 and Biology. I went to classes four nights a week and studied during the day, spending the weekends with Ed as well as with friends and family.

One afternoon, about four months later, I was sitting in the living room and reading when I felt this flutter in my stomach. At first I thought I was just imagining things and ignored it, but then a few minutes later I felt the flutter again. Oh my God, this was the baby moving! I was so excited that I could not contain myself. I called my friend Pat, who had just had her baby, and she confirmed that yes, this was the sensation of the baby moving. I then called Ed and told him all about it; I wished he could experience this most miraculous feeling for himself.

This feeling was the first of many that would continue to arise as the baby developed. I loved being pregnant and the feeling of the life moving within my body. I would just sit and feel the baby's movement and thank God for this miracle.

I would feel the baby move around during my classes and wondered what effect they would have on the life growing inside of me. I also read my textbook on maternity nursing so I could learn what was happening to my body and the baby's growth and development stage by stage—at this time, there were no other books available on this subject.

I did not see my mother and father too much during this time because I was busy with school and studies. I did frequently call my mother to let her know how I was feeling and to see how she and my family were doing. She was excited for me, and I was looking forward to seeing how my three-year-old brother would react when he got to see his nephew, who would be so close to him in age. My feelings of anger toward my mother were softening as I saw her excitement about being a grandmother.

I was lucky to carry the baby easily without becoming too large. My doctor was concerned that I might get a condition called toxemia due to my initial weight gain, so he had me write down everything I ate and drank. Thankfully, because I was so conscious of my weight to start with, I only gained twenty-three pounds by the time my due date arrived.

While my pregnancy was wonderful overall, there were some moments of stress and worry. On November 23, 1963, I was taking a break from studying to have lunch and watch a soap opera when the program was interrupted by a news broadcast. President Kennedy had been shot, and they were not sure if he would live or die. Everyone in our nation and around the world was in shock. Throughout the rest of the weekend, all we could do was to sit glued to the TV and watch the events unfold.

I had achieved the American Dream—I was married to a great-looking, guy, had a baby on the way, and was back in school—but now all those dreams seemed to pale as the world began to change. I do not recall ever having such a sense of gloom and doom as I did that weekend. What kind of world would my baby be born into? What kind of country would we become now? It was a sad time. Today, in 2019, I feel the same way I did in 1963 because of the increasing gun violence that we are experiencing, although my concern is now for both my children and my grandchildren.

Valentine's Day came, and I awoke that morning with the knowledge that I was going to have a baby; I was having a scheduled induction because that was the only way the obstetrician performed births, although you had to be at a certain level of dilation when you arrived. It was a cold, dreary winter morning as Ed and I left to drive to the hospital in Brooklyn. I remember being calm and ready to have my baby.

Births were different back in those days. Fathers were not allowed in the birthing rooms and there was no consideration of anyone except the physician and nurses. Mothers, including myself, would be given anesthesia and be put to sleep while the baby was born. Today, natural childbirth is common and the mother can invite several family members into the room to share in the birth of the baby. Many mothers choose to have a spinal injection to ease the pain of labor and childbirth, allowing them to be fully awake for the birth of their baby. I got to witness this type of birthing experience when my daughter gave birth to her own daughter, Emily, and again when my son's wife, Jen, gave birth to both Benjamin and Ashley. It was a beautiful moment to be a part of.

Patrick Edward Phelan was born at noon on February 14, 1964—Patrick after his paternal great-grandfather and Edward after his dad. He was the first grandchild on both sides of the family, and his arrival into the world was heralded by an enormous amount of love. He had a head of dark black hair and brown eyes, and I couldn't stop staring at him. He was perfect. It was amazing to finally meet this little baby that had been growing inside of me, and my heart swelled with love for him. I was now a mother of a beautiful baby boy, and I vowed to always love and protect him with all of my heart.

My mother offered to come help us with the baby after he was born, and I agreed. My parents were so wonderful to me while I was pregnant with Patrick. They had given me a baby shower and helped us to get the basics we needed. After all of this support, I felt that it would be beneficial to have my mother around to help me transition into being a mother myself.

Two days after she arrived, I found myself wanting to be alone with my baby. I was getting irritated at everything she did, such as the fact that she would shake out wet towels in the kitchen and the way she wrapped the baby. I finally had to tell her that while I knew she meant well, I thought it would be better for me to be alone. Thankfully, she said she understood how I felt, and she was okay with going home as she needed to take care of my four-year-old little brother.

Ed was thrilled with being a father. He loved to hold Patrick in his arms, and he could not help but tell everyone he was the father of a little boy. Patrick was a good baby who most nights slept for long periods of time, to the point that we would get up in the middle of the night to make sure he was still breathing. Ed and I could not get over his perfect features, his beautiful smile, and his adorable coos. It was a very happy time in our lives.

There was a slight wrinkle in this wonderful experience. When I was in the hospital with Patrick, I noticed that I had a problem with water getting into my right eye when I washed my face. I thought it was probably a side effect from the anesthesia that would go away on its own, so I said nothing to anyone at the time. However, when the symptoms persisted several days after I came home, I finally called my doctor.

I was quickly diagnosed with Bell's palsy. The right side of my face was paralyzed—I could not get my right eye all the way shut, and my smile only went to the left side of my face. The cause was unknown, but they thought that I could have caught a chill or that the way they held my head during childbirth may have created this. Regardless of the cause, I just wanted to get better. I could not understand how this could have happened to me, a healthy twenty-two-year-old. I was supposed to be a bridesmaid in Pat and Jerry's wedding party six weeks later; how could I do that with only one side of my face working? By the time the wedding date arrived, I decided to go ahead and participate in the happy celebration in spite of my face not being fully recovered, and I had a wonderful time.

After my diagnosis, I was put on a heavy dose of steroids for six weeks. About eight weeks later my face was finally back to normal, and I was so happy being a mother that the problem was quickly forgotten.

# Chapter 10

## Another Move

Four months after Patrick was born, Ed and I were asked to leave our rented apartment. The people who owned the house were an older couple, and they had difficulty listening to the baby cry. We found a one-bedroom apartment in Fresh Meadows, New York, which was only minutes from my in-laws and our friends, but unfortunately this new place was not furnished. We had to buy some new furniture, but we did not have much money at this time. We managed to purchase a new bedroom set, a crib, and a few necessary pieces for the apartment, which were just enough to get us by until we could afford the rest.

Shortly after we moved, I began taking a night course in Sociology. This allowed me to be with Patrick during the day, squeezing in my studying when he took his naps, while Ed was home with him in the evenings. Life was busy for us as new parents, but I was happy to be challenged and working toward my nursing degree.

Patrick was our love and joy, and Ed and I marveled at each and every milestone. Our hearts filled with love at his first steps and his first words of "Dada" and "Mama." Patrick was a delightful child who made motherhood better than I could have ever imagined, and Ed was a wonderful and caring father who enjoyed his role as a dad and his time with Patrick when I was in my evening classes.

I continued taking two classes in the fall of 1964—English Composition and Literature—and my mother offered to watch Patrick two days a week while I was in school. I would drive Patrick to my parents' home an hour away and then picked him up after class so I could return home to make dinner for Ed and myself. Guy, who was only four years older than Patrick, loved to see and spend time with him, and Patrick was always excited and happy to see him too. My mom loved to take them both to the park, where they enjoyed playing on the swings and visiting the ducks that were in the pond. My mother was happy to have time with Patrick and our relationship was good at this time, although we did not spend a lot of time together because I was busy with classes and motherhood.

In October 1964, our lives once again changed. Ed came home and said, "I need to talk with you after we put Patrick down to sleep for the night." I felt a sense of dread wash over me; it was unusual for him to be so serious.

After Patrick was asleep, we went into the small living room and sat down across from one another. Ed informed me that he had been promoted to the Director of Sales for the Guardian Life Insurance Company, which meant we would need to move to Chicago, Illinois. We were both excited about this promotion, and there was no question that we would accept this offer; it was a crucial step for us, both financially and in regards to Ed's future in the company. However, I also told him that we would need to find a way to transfer my schooling to a college in the area; I didn't want to give up on my dream of being a nurse again.

A month after we received this news, my paternal grandmother went into a diabetic coma at age seventy-nine. I was so sad to see her in the hospital, attached to tubes and a respirator in an effort to simply keep her alive. Sadly, she never woke up. Patrick and I attended her funeral, along with my parents and many other family members.

After she passed, Ed and I sat down together to find a place to live and to make a plan that was satisfactory for the both of us. We decided that Ed would move first so he could find an apartment for us and get caught up in his new position, and then I would follow with Patrick once I had finished my semester and could transfer to a school there. Ed's company had agreed to pay for him to come back and visit one weekend per month until I was able to move, which made the distance much more manageable. Ed moved to Chicago in November 1964 and began searching for an apartment while Patrick and I lived with my in-laws until I finished my classes. Ed found a beautiful two-bedroom apartment on the ground floor of a new building, and the three of us moved to Downers Grove, Illinois, in February 1965. We left Flushing, New York, and all our family and friends behind to embark on this unknown adventure together.

Surprisingly, I found that living away from our families was a delight. We had been constantly busy with family activities— for example, we were always expected to attend a family brunch at the Phelan home every Sunday. Now that we had left behind those commitments, we were able to focus on ourselves and on Patrick.

Because of our recent move, I did not attend school that spring semester. Instead, I decided to go back to work to help pay for our new life and apartment. I applied for a night position as a nurse aide because Ed would be home to take care of Patrick. I never thought I would take another position as a nurse aide after my bad experience with that first summer job, but I was not qualified to do anything else in the health care field. We needed extra money, and I wanted to help out with our finances.

Going back to work was much more difficult than I expected. I had to complete a two-week orientation that ran during the day, and I had to leave Patrick with a babysitter from 6:00 AM to 4:00 PM every day for two weeks while I was completing the orientation. It was painful to have to wake him up and bring him to the sitter's home. The sitter was a very nice middle-aged woman, and I had to trust she was a good person that would take great care of our son. The fact it was only for two weeks was the silver lining.

I thought I would be okay after the orientation finished and I switched to night shifts, but I still found it painful to leave Patrick each night. I would get home at 8:00 AM, just before Ed left for work, and while I was ready to go to bed, Patrick would be just waking up from his night's sleep. I forced myself to stay awake because I knew I could sleep when he took his early afternoon nap. Luckily I had just turned twenty-three, so I was able to adapt to this difficult schedule fairly well. I kept thinking positive by focusing on making money to help pay our rent, and on the fact that I would soon return to school to finish my nursing degree. However, after four months of working the night shift, I again developed several bald spots on the top of my head due to stress. Ed and I agreed that I would quit my position as a nurse aide in June 1965, which fell shortly before we went back to New York to visit our family for a wonderful two-week vacation.

We went back to New York for another family visit during the summer of 1966, and I decided to take two four-week night courses that were prerequisites for my nursing degree, Art Appreciation and Child Development, at the college I attended while living in New York. Taking these classes in New York meant that my mother and father could take care of Patrick while I was in classes as opposed to leaving him with a stranger. Ed did not mind my being away at this time because he knew how important my family was to Patrick, and because he was busy with work. My mother agreed to help out with Patrick because she missed seeing him, and I knew that he would enjoy the time with Guy and my parents. However, I soon learned that this arrangement was less than ideal. The courses were very intense in order for them to be completed in such a short time frame, and I had a limited amount of time to study. I also had Patrick with me during the day, which affected my options for where I could get my work done. One day, my mother and I got into an argument. I had a final paper that was due, and I needed to use the kitchen to complete it as there was nowhere else I could sit down with the typewriter. It was a day when my mother and her friend Edna usually had their weekly lunch together, and I politely asked if they could meet another day so I could get my work done. My mom's response was to brush me off and tell me that I would just have to find another place to go, but that was not an option for me. I was stressed and angry. I called my mother-in-law and asked if it was okay if Patrick and I stayed with her for the next two weeks so I could finish the summer classes, and then I left.

In retrospect, I can see that I was still trying to get my mother's support in obtaining my nursing degree. They say the definition of insanity is doing the same thing over and over again and expecting different results, and I guess I met that criteria. No matter how old I was, no matter what I had accomplished, I was still seeking the approval and support of my mother and father. And even though our relationship had improved in recent years, it only took a moment like this one to send me right back to that kitchen in Massapequa Park, hearing my mom tell me that I would never accomplish my dream.

# Chapter 11

## A Daughter Is Born

As we entered into the year 1967, our lives were going very well. Ed was enjoying his role as the District Manager of the Guardian Life Insurance Company and Patrick was a fun and curious three-year-old. We went back to New York twice a year to see our family, although my relationship with my parents was now fairly superficial. As for me, well, I had some exciting news to share.

One day in January, Ed had barely gotten through the front door of our apartment after work when I blurted out, "Guess what? You are going to be a father again!" He put down his briefcase and rushed over to give me a hug with a big smile on his face. I told him I had gone to the doctor earlier that day to confirm the pregnancy, and the baby was due in September. We decided not to say anything to Patrick yet since he was too young to comprehend what was happening; we had not been around any other friends or family who were pregnant or had recently had a baby, so he had nothing to relate this news to. We did call our families, though, and they were so happy to be grandparents again.

Since our family was expanding, we decided to purchase a two-story, three-bedroom brick home on a tree-lined street in an established area of Downers Grove. After visiting many friends who lived in similar neighborhoods over the years, I had dreamed that I would live in an area like this. The house had an indoor porch and kitchen that overlooked a large backyard. The first floor included two bedrooms, one off the dining room and another off the living room. The fireplace in the living room was encased between built-in bookshelves which created a warm and welcoming feel. The second floor was solely comprised of a huge master bedroom with a bathroom, and we also had a full basement and two-car detached garage. The house was immaculate, having previously been owned by an older couple who had lived there for most of their married lives. There was an older neighbor with a young boy close to Patrick's age, and our other neighbors, Dorothy and Jim Leach, had older children in grade school who were wonderful babysitters for us. It was the perfect first home for us, and we planned on moving in August 1967.

Around this time, Ed and I decided to send Patrick to a private preschool two days a week to give him some experience with other children before the baby was born and to get a head start on school prior to him entering kindergarten. I had heard of an excellent school called Avery Coonley that was located in a beautiful wooded setting and had small class sizes. It only accepted children who were in the superior to gifted IQ ranges so Patrick had to be tested before he could be accepted, and he did well. The three of us were experiencing several life changes in our own individual ways: my pregnancy, becoming homeowners, our move, attending preschool, and anticipating a new baby within a month after the move.

During this time, I had taken a semester off from classes

because we knew we would be moving into a new home and so I wouldn't have time to focus on my studies. Instead, I spent some time exploring other activities. I played bridge in a women and couples group. I enjoyed the challenge, and my bridge partner Kay Selfridge and I won the intermediate women's tournament. I also learned to sew because I thought it would be fun to create something. I even made a green pregnancy dress that I loved wearing, but I stopped sewing after that because I realized my interests were more academic than creative. I returned to school the summer before the baby was due and took a course in Microbiology.

The morning of September 9, 1967, arrived and we were finally going to meet our new baby. Ed and I drove to Saint Joseph's Hospital in Chicago where I would be induced; in the three years since I had last given birth, very little had changed.

When I arrived at the hospital at 6:00 AM, I was met by the nurses and medical team. After the initial history and physical examination by the resident doctor, I was placed in the delivery area to wait for my personal obstetrician to come and start the induction procedure. He did not arrive until close to 11:00 AM, and by the time he arrived I was upset that I had been waiting for so long. Shortly after his arrival I was given Pitocin, a drug used to induce labor, and I was then given anesthesia once the contractions started in order to put me to sleep during the birth process. They started the process at noon, and Liz was born at 4:15 PM.

I was placed in a recovery room while I was still asleep. As the anesthesia wore off, the nurse saw I was waking up and came over to check my vital signs. Unsure whether I was awake or dreaming, I asked if I'd had my baby, and she said yes. I immediately started to wonder if something was wrong.

Why didn't she tell me the sex of my baby? I was becoming anxious and concerned. I asked where my baby was.

The nurse looked at me and said, "The baby is in the nursery, and you can see her later."

I was so anxious that I did not fully hear what the nurse said. I asked, "What did I have?"

"It is a girl."

I had a girl! I did not think I would be so lucky to have both a son and daughter so easily. As I sat alone in the recovery room, I wondered if Ed had gotten to see her.

They gave Elizabeth Ann Phelan to me a few hours later. I looked at her beautiful face and her dark black hair and brown eyes, and she was perfect. She looked so much like her brother Patrick, except her facial features were more delicate. I relaxed back into my bed on the maternity floor and just held her close to me and relished the moment. It was still common practice at this time to bring the baby back to the nursery for the seven days the mom was hospitalized. Liz was brought to me for the frequent bottle feedings throughout the day, and if I was up to it I could walk down the hall and see her in her bassinet from the large window of the nursery.

While I was so excited to finally meet my daughter, I missed Patrick. This was the longest I had been away from him, and I found that leaving him—even for such a joyous occasion—was painful. I was able to talk with Patrick on the phone, but it wasn't the same as being able to see him and hold him. My only consolation was knowing that Ed would be with him each evening after work, and that my friend Kay Selfridge was with him during the day.

After Liz was born, Ed and I were busy settling into being parents to two young children. I talked to my parents on occasion, and they were looking forward to our visit back to New York for Christmas so that they could meet their new granddaughter. The relationship between my parents and myself continued to stay cordial. I was always the one to call home and the one to travel so we could visit, which was expected due to my parents' financial struggles. We made sure to go to New York twice a year to see them so that my children would have the opportunity to know their grandparents, as well as my brother Guy. I had lost touch with Sonny and his wife before Ed and I got married—we had not been close since childhood, and we simply drifted apart.

I always appreciated that we were able to connect and bond with our families; I wanted my children to have the same sense of a strong family foundation growing up that I experienced with my paternal grandparents. I was determined to give my children the best aspects of my own childhood, the ones that I still look back on fondly to this day.

# Chapter 12

## What Is Wrong with Me?

"You should be so happy! You have a wonderful husband, two beautiful children, and a nice home," said my friend Kay. But, for reasons beyond my knowledge, I was not happy.

I loved my children and adored our new home and neighborhood. Patrick was enjoying his preschool and seemed to like having a little sister, except that he no longer ate vegetables after she was born—I think this was his way of rebelling against the changes in his life. Patrick seemed to enjoy playing with Liz and making her laugh, although I did once discover him using her as a stepping stone. Thankfully, it did not take much for him to realize this was not how to play with your sister.

Liz also seemed to adore her brother and loved to play with him. She was an easy baby to care for, sleeping through the whole night almost from the first day we brought her home. We put a record player in her room so we could play classical music because I had read that this was calming for babies. She seemed to love it, and she would fall asleep shortly after we put the music on. I love that she still enjoys classical music today, and every time I hear her play it I'm brought back to those precious moments.

We flew back to New York shortly after Liz was born so we could share our new addition with our family. My mother-in-law also flew out to Illinois when Liz was about nine months old to visit us in our home. Pat and Jerry were the godparents for both of my children, and they also flew out so they could be a part of Liz's baptism. It was wonderful to have family visit us and see where we were living after being here for three years.

Life was good on the surface, but deep down I was struggling with an unhappiness that I could not identify or understand. During the first few months after Liz was born, I was getting dizzy spells and felt a terrible sense of dread almost every day. The worst of these spells happened while driving on the freeway with my children in the back seat. I started to feel dizzy and disoriented and thought I might black out, and I was terrified. What would happen to them if I lost consciousness? I pulled over to the side of the road and took a few deep breaths. There were no cell phones or any way to let anyone know I was in trouble, so I had no other option than to just try to calm myself down. After a few minutes, I regained my composure enough to drive home, continuing to take deep breaths and telling myself I had to pull it together to get my kids home safe.

Unfortunately, the dizzy spells became more frequent and I began to fear leaving the house. I was losing control! I finally hit a breaking point and called our doctor for a physical exam. I wanted to know why I was feeling unhappy and what was causing my dizzy spells, but he just told me that I had anxiety and prescribed Valium. I felt he was treating me like an object and was not really listening to me, but I did not have the energy to dispute his diagnosis. I took the prescription and decided I would at least try it and see if it would help. After all, I had nothing to lose—my anxiety was increasing every day.

The medication did not help, and soon these spells were truly getting out of control. I would go to the supermarket to pick up a few items, and as I walked up and down the aisles I would get dizzy and feel overwhelmed by all of the food choices. I would feel sick and run out of the store immediately before I passed out. Ed knew of my symptoms but did not understand what was going on with me, nor did I. Unfortunately, the symptoms only continued to progress.

In the spring of 1968, Ed had planned on going on a business trip to Monterey, California. I was supposed to go with him, so several months before the conference I hired a woman to babysit so she could get to know our children and would be comfortable in our week-long absence. I was looking forward to seeing California, and to having time alone as a couple.

Unfortunately, a week before the conference the babysitter had to cancel due to back problems. I was so upset. After all of the planning and anticipation, I was unable to go on this long-planned trip. When I told Ed, he just brushed it off and said it was no problem, he would be back in a couple of days. I was upset with his indifference and disappointed that I wouldn't be able to join him for a vacation together, and the more upset I became, the worse the dizzy spells got.

After hearing about my predicament, my friend Kay suggested that I see a psychiatrist. At first I was very resistant to the idea because I thought only crazy people went to see one. While Ed was away, though, I gave it a bit more thought. I asked myself, what would I say if I were to see a psychiatrist? Right away, the answer was clear: I wanted to go back to school.

I had decided not to take classes after Liz was born so I

could focus my time and attention on my new daughter, and on helping Patrick adjust to our changed family dynamic. I also had completed the required college prerequisites for the nursing program, and so the next step was to take the nursing classes. These classes required at least two full days of working and traveling to different medical centers for on-the-job experience, plus a half day of classroom time. These classes had to be taken in succession over the course of two years; there was no option of taking the nursing classes piecemeal like I had been doing with the elective courses. I needed to be sure that I had this time available and had a babysitter around to care for my children.

Around this time, I also started to fantasize about having an affair. Not with anyone in particular, mind you, but these thoughts were unacceptable to me. It was becoming more and more clear to me that I needed to get to the bottom of where these negative thoughts were coming from.

When Ed returned after his business trip, something within me had changed. He brought me back a pair of salt and pepper shakers, and I threw them against the stairs. I was hurt and frustrated that he did not care that I could not join him on the trip, and the gift of the salt and pepper shakers was demeaning to me. They felt like thoughtless, impersonal tokens that you pick up at the airport, and I think they were the straw that broke the camel's back. I knew I could not continue to feel out of control and started to question my relationship with Ed. I told Ed about everything that was going on—my unhappiness, the dizzy spells, and my anger that he didn't care if I was with him at the conference—and said that I wanted to see a psychiatrist so I could find the underlying cause for what was happening. Ed didn't seem to understand the importance of what I was saying, but he gave me some money and told me to do what I wanted with it.

I made my way to Dr. Robert D's office a week later, full of anxiety. This was an unknown world to me. I did not know what to expect since I knew of only one other friend who had been to a psychiatrist, but we did not talk much about it.

I entered into a small waiting room with two side chairs and a table with magazines. Shortly after I arrived, the door to the inner office opened, and I saw a handsome man with dark hair and brown eyes that were warm and welcoming. I was surprised by how young he looked, but I was happy because he seemed to be more approachable than perhaps a much older man would be. As we entered his small, comfortable office with a black leather sofa and two leather chairs, I started to relax.

Dr. D was soft-spoken and gentle. He asked me questions about my background before asking me why I was there and what I wanted to get out of the session. I started with the current physical symptoms I was experiencing and said that I wanted to understand why they were happening and to not rely on anti-anxiety medication to mask the real problem. He agreed with my goals, and we made several appointments for the next few weeks due to my crisis situation. It was a bit daunting to take this first big step and admit there was something wrong with me, but I left that first session feeling hopeful that I would find some answers.

After a few sessions, Dr. D stated that the dizzy spells were due to my defense mechanisms being lowered because I had a daughter, causing unconscious thoughts and feelings that I found unacceptable to break through into my consciousness. In essence, having a daughter brought up the unresolved relationship I had with my mother. I believe each person that comes into our lives helps us fulfill our life lessons, and it seemed as if Liz would be my teacher in helping me resolve the relationship between my mother and me. My unconscious reason for this anxiety was that I did not want to repeat the negative mother-daughter relationship that I had seen between my mother and maternal grandmother, and between my mother and myself.

My maternal grandmother was always angry with one family member or another. She would play off one child against the other and try to persuade them to take her side of the argument. Often the result was that one or more of the siblings would not be talking to my grandmother, or to one another. This family dynamic had repeated itself throughout my life. My mother and grandmother were always in conflict with one another over the most mundane issues; it was as if anger was the only way they knew how to gain some separation and independence from one another. This is common with teenagers who are separating from their parents toward independence, and they seemed to be stuck at this level of maturity.

Once I became a young teen myself, I would shake my head and roll my eyes whenever my mother told me that she was no longer talking to my grandmother or to one of her own siblings. This was not the kind of relationship I wanted for my daughter and son, but it would take several years of therapy for me to understand this insight and to come to a place of forgiveness.

I also wanted to talk to Dr. D about the difficulty I had being intimate with Ed—I had yet to become fully comfortable with having sex. Through these sessions, I discovered that finding those naked photos under my parents' bed had had a bigger impact than I'd realized. I had been too young to understand what those photos were about, but I still ended up comparing my underdeveloped body to what I saw. There were other incidents that came into play as well, including hearing that my mother had come out in a negligee in front of her male and female friends during a party in our house when I was seven and seeing my dad photograph my mom in seductive poses when I was eight. As a result of these events, I associated sex with all of the negative qualities of my mother and developed issues with my body image. It was difficult to overcome these traumatic events and move on to become the loving sexual partner I thought I should be for Ed.

While it may sound as if I'm blaming my mother for my reaction to these events, that is not how I feel about the situation. Another child may have been totally indifferent to this experience; I just happened to be very sensitive to this type of influence.

After I had gone to a few sessions, Ed started to express an interest in attending these appointments with me. However, the therapist did not think it was in my best interest and suggested that Ed see another therapist if he wanted to see someone himself. Of course, improving himself is not why he wanted to come to my sessions—Ed thought himself to be perfect, and that any issues I had existed solely within myself. He only wanted to go to the sessions with me so he could understand what he could do to fix me. This attitude from Ed was one of the many reasons that my feelings toward him began to erode.

Unfortunately for our relationship, I became stronger as a woman through these sessions and began to look at myself in a new light. I started to evaluate my talents, skills, and dreams and truly make them a priority. I was not only able to take classes and be the mother of my two young children, but I could also be the "good wife" who was involved in my husband's career and attended social activities with our neighborhood friends, had gourmet dinner parties, and played tennis twice a week. I returned to nursing school in the fall of 1969 with a newfound determination and the support of my wonderful therapist.

I remember a night in 1970 where I was sitting in our living room in my favorite olive-green velvet chair and studying for my nursing exam. Patrick and Liz were asleep, and Ed was watching television in our family room. I was having difficulty reading, so I stopped and looked up from my book. My struggles with my studies were reminding me of my marital struggles, and the thought crossed my mind that I needed to leave my husband of six years. I was completely caught off guard by this idea. How could I do this? Where would I go? Or live? How would I finish my nursing degree? The idea was frightening, but I couldn't keep denying that I no longer loved my husband. Noticing that my thoughts were getting away from me, I told myself that I couldn't do this right now and decided to discuss it with my therapist. Divorce was out of the question, at least at this time in my life.

In 1971, we bought a new home in an upscale neighborhood of Downers Grove. On the outside, we were a happy and successful family. On the inside, though, I was struggling to keep my marriage intact.

That same year, I finally obtained my associate degree in nursing and started working two days a week as a registered nurse on the medical floor of a large teaching hospital in Chicago. I felt a deep pride and satisfaction within myself for finally obtaining this degree. I did not have the support and congratulations from either my husband or parents— something that I had long known not to expect—but I did have the support and congratulations from my therapist and my best friend Suzanne, who also graduated with me. I had finally achieved my dream, and I once again felt good about myself as a woman and mother.

By 1973 I had been going to psychotherapy for four years, and I ended up with a very positive transference relationship with my psychiatrist. He lived in the same town as we did and belonged to the same swim and tennis club. Over the years, as he helped support me with my goal of becoming a nurse, we also became involved in the same social events in Downers Grove, something that could be seen as blurring the boundaries between doctor and patient.

Eventually, this transference relationship began to cross the line. Ed and I were involved in a dance group that would meet about four times a year, and Dr. D and his wife would attend these events as well. I loved getting dressed up to attend these formal dances so I could show off to Dr. D. As Ed and I danced, I would make eye contact and flirt with Dr. D, even though I knew this was not the proper doctor-patient relationship. Nothing more came from this flirtation, and later that year Dr. D told me I would have to see another psychiatrist as he could no longer see me as a patient. I eventually found out from the psychoanalyst that he referred me to that Dr. D had a positive counter-transference towards me. He was very professional, though, and ended the relationship before it became detrimental to both of us.

I continued working on trying to save my marriage, although after struggling in our relationship for ten years my feelings for Ed were difficult to deny. When we returned home from a social event and closed the door to the outside world, I felt a vacant emptiness between us. Ed's social, flamboyant self would disappear as soon as we got home. He became silent, and we wouldn't talk beyond the necessary everyday conversations about our daily activities, our children, and what time we were having dinner.

I believe the waning relationship I had with Ed caused us both to be the best parents we could be. I had a close relationship with my daughter and son which was nothing like the angst I had experienced with my own mother. My focus in therapy was to ensure that my relationship with Patrick and Liz would always be a loving, supportive, and open one. I worked hard at looking within myself to live a conscious life and try to understand my relationship with my mother so I did not repeat the same dysfunctional pattern I grew to know.

Unfortunately, Ed and I were simply growing apart. We kept busy with our children, who we both adored, and we enjoyed attending their after-school activities of baseball and football for Patrick and swim team and softball for Elizabeth. They became the focus of our lives while our marriage was slowly dying.

Pat and Liz

# Chapter 13

## "I Wish I Had Done..."

Each day that I went to work on the medical floor after graduating from the associate nursing program, I awoke with a tightness in my stomach. I needed to wake up at 5:00 AM to be in Chicago by 6:45 AM so I could get the night duty report from the charge nurse before starting my shift at 7:00 AM. Waking up this early, it was easy to think about hiding under my covers and going back to sleep. I thought to myself, *why am I doing this?* We did not need the money, and I had a four-year-old daughter and a seven-year-old son who were depending on me, as well as their dad, to be there for them.

As new graduates, my classmates and I were encouraged to work on a medical floor for at least a year to practice our newly-acquired skills. Once we accomplished this experience, we could then go on to practice in the area of our interest. In my heart of hearts, I initially wanted to go straight into psychiatric nursing because it consisted primarily of patients with psychiatric problems, not medical, so I felt that practicing my skills on a medical floor may not be useful. I must admit, though, that as a new graduate, I was very happy I went to work on the medical unit as it helped me become quite confident in my nursing skills. This experience was also valuable later in my career because psychiatric patients were often admitted with medical problems as well.

My first choice of location to practice nursing was Rush Presbyterian St. Luke's Hospital in Chicago—known today as Rush Medical Center—which was a large medical center and teaching hospital. Each morning, all of the nursing staff, registered nurses, vocational nurses, and nurse aides would meet in the staff room to hear the night report of each patient on the forty-bed unit. It was the team leader's responsibility to assign the care of each patient to a staff person according to the severity of the patient's disease or illness. The population of this unit ranged from the indigent to the fairly wealthy, and we dealt with a variety of health conditions including bleeding ulcers, diabetes, heart symptoms, emphysema, cancer, motorcycle injuries, dialysis, and drug overdoses. I later learned this floor was called "the snake pit" because of the many medical challenges that were experienced on this one unit. This was the perfect place to learn and master my nursing skills.

Because I only worked two days a week my colleagues often assigned me the most difficult patients. My first impression was they were being mean, but in looking back I believe that the full-time workers just needed a break from these tough patients.

My anxiety rose every time I went to work because I never knew to whom I would be assigned that day and what medical challenges I would have to face. However, once I arrived on the unit and got my assignment, I would forget about myself and my anxiety and focus on my patient—thinking about how I would want to be treated if I was in their situation helped me overcome my fear. My daily nursing assignments usually consisted of giving a total bed bath if the patient was unable to care for themselves, a back rub, and a change of bed sheets for six to seven patients each day. I strove to be a competent nurse since it had taken years of part-time study to get my degree and I was not yet confident in my newly-acquired skills.

Shortly after starting on the unit, I was assigned to the medication room for the first time. I was then responsible for giving out all the medications for the forty patients on the unit as well as setting up the intravenous solutions and antibiotics if the physician had ordered them. There was a written index of all the patients' names and medications and the time each patient was to receive them, and I had to ensure they were kept up to date. Today a pharmacist would be in charge of this, but back then it was the duty of a registered nurse.

I truly dreaded the days I was assigned to the medication room. I worried about giving the wrong medication to the wrong patient, and this fear caused me to be obsessive about checking the name of the patient and what medication they were prescribed. By the end of my shift I would be exhausted, but I was always relieved that I did not harm anyone. I far preferred the days that I was in charge of patient care as I found it to be very satisfying. The look on my patients' faces after my care—whether it was a back rub, getting a glass of water, or just listening as I cared for them—made me feel as if I was making a difference in their day.

I believe that my patients were a gift to me, because they taught me many lessons. One patient I had cared for was just over forty years old and had a condition called myasthenia gravis which paralyzed her from the neck down to her toes. As I bathed her, she began telling me about all the things that she had not yet accomplished and wished she had been able to do.

Listening to her made me realize how short life can be and that we should not take our health for granted. The message I came away with from this beautiful soul was that I did not want to be on my death bed someday saying, "I wish I had done…"

Another important lesson came about four months after I started working, when I was assigned to an eighteen-year-old who was in a coma due to a drug overdose. He was on a ventilator and we weren't sure how long he would survive. I was told that his family had been informed of his hospitalization and would be visiting him later that morning, and that this would be my only patient for the day due to the amount of nursing care he required.

I anxiously walked into his room and assessed what care was needed. I started to get his bed bath ready and obtain the relevant items to ensure I would not to have to leave the room unnecessarily. I checked his vitals, looking for signs of an infection, and I also checked his IV to ensure the antibiotics were dripping in the amount that had been prescribed. As I worked, I observed this handsome young male lying in a coma and wondered what circumstances had brought him to be here.

At lunchtime I was relieved by another nurse so I could take my break, and upon my return I was surprised to see that the plug to the ventilator had been removed and the patient had died. I was in shock and dismayed that someone had actually pulled the plug on this young man. I immediately went to the nurse who had taken over during my lunch and asked, "How did this happen? Who did this?" I did not get any answers, and it was implied that I should not ask any more questions.

The patient's wife arrived shortly after, and since I could not find the doctor who was caring for him or the charge nurse of the unit, I had to tell her that her husband had passed away. It felt so surreal. I walked into the lounge and this petite young pregnant woman with dark hair and an anxious face started to get up and walk towards me. I directed her to the sofa nearby and we sat down together; thankfully, we were the only ones in the room. I broke the news as gently as I could, and she looked at me and started to shake her head and wail, "No! No! It cannot be true! I did not get to tell him I loved him! I did not get to tell him I loved him!" I did my best to keep my emotions in check as all I wanted to do was cry with her. Finally, the charge nurse came after hearing her grief and offered her a sedative so that she would not faint.

We went back to the room so she could see her husband. As soon as we entered, she ran to his bedside and threw herself over his body, crying and stating over and over how much she loved him. It was so emotional and painful. My stomach was in knots, and I felt helpless and overwhelmed in grief for her. All I could do was take a deep breath, look up at the ceiling as she wailed, and be there with her and support her as much as I could.

Shortly after, the patient's mother and two older brothers came into the room. They were devastated and crying in disbelief. Suddenly, the older brother also flung himself over his brother's body and cried out "I am so sorry" over and over. I learned soon after that he had started the patient on drugs. This was one of the most emotionally difficult situations that I have ever experienced. There was nothing I could say to help this family who were engulfed with this tragic loss of their loved one.

As the family left the room after saying goodbye, I noticed that the older brother could not walk. He was being held up by his mother and brother with his legs buckling underneath him. The patient was in peace, but his brother had been left debilitated by his grief and guilt.

The lesson I learned from this sad and traumatic experience was the profound sense of not saying "I love you" enough. I will now always tell my family and loved ones that I love them, and I will never go to bed angry with my husband. Life is too short, and we never know when our last day will come.

# Chapter 14

## Who Do You Think You Are ?

After working on this unit for four months, I had come to admire and respect Shirley Butz, the head nurse. Shirley was a slender, attractive woman in her early forties with gray streaks running through her dark hair. She was an excellent role model for me because of her clinical expertise in providing excellent patient care, and I felt intimidated by her because of her exceptional nursing skills and her no-nonsense personality. I respected her extensive knowledge of every aspect of patient care, from the simple to the complex. No matter what the diagnosis was, Shirley had an answer!

She called me into her office one day and asked me to sit down on the only chair next to her small desk. After exchanging a few pleasantries, she said, "I asked you to come in today because I want to tell you how impressed I am with your work. On the days you are working, I would like to have you be the team leader on the unit." The team leader works directly under the head nurse and gives out the daily assignments of patient care.

I could not have been any happier than I was hearing those words from her. I was honored to receive such a positive professional opinion of my ability and to be offered this kind of responsibility so soon after I graduated, especially since I was working only two days a week.

I started my new position a week later. I now went on morning rounds with the attending doctors, Shirley, the residents, and the interns. These rounds gave each of us a total picture of the concerns of each patient and what care they needed, which helped me determine the most appropriate staff to assign each patient to. I was also responsible for looking at the doctor's orders on each patient after the morning rounds and then communicating any changes in the patient's treatment to the staff nurse and the medicine nurse. After I listened to the night nurse give her report of the patient's health status, I then assigned the six nursing staff their patients for the day depending on the level of nursing skill required to care for them. At the end of the day, each of the nurses on my team would report to me to give a summary of the care that was provided and communicate any concerns that needed to be passed on to the next shift.

There were two other registered nurses on the unit that had graduated the same year that I did. One of them was a fellow nursing student who I did not know very well, and the other nurse I did not know at all. They were both full-time employees and I sensed they were envious of my part-time work, but I tried to ignore when they excluded me at lunch time and during coffee breaks. I was not there to make friends; my focus was on developing my nursing skills and on patient care. Thankfully, the other staff members were great to work with and very professional, especially Shirley.

During my morning medical rounds, I began to notice that

the doctors were very gracious and friendly toward me, more so than the other nursing staff. Eventually, I found out why. There was an attending physician on the unit named Doctor Phelan—the same last name as my married name. We were all required to wear name badges, and as I started working closer with the doctors on the unit, my name became more prominent. The residents and interns thought I was Dr. Phelan's wife, which explained the deference I received from them. This was amusing to me because my mother had told me that a doctor would never marry me once they knew who I was, and here I was with a whole medical unit that believed I was married to one. It certainly was an odd coincidence.

In spite of my developing position as a nurse on the medical unit, I was still suffering anxiety each morning when I had to leave my children to go to work. My son Patrick was eight and a half years old at this time and an excellent student, and he did not seem to be affected by my work. However, my daughter, who was five years of age, would cry each morning, complaining of stomach aches and claiming that I needed to stay home. I struggled so hard to balance my need to be there for my daughter and also fulfill my need to be someone that she would be proud to say was her mom. If I had not maintained my therapy appointments, I do not know how I could have handled not only my dear daughter's and husband's reactions to my driving desire to be a nurse, but also the reactions I received from my fellow nurses.

Shortly after I became the team leader, I had assigned four patients to Nurse C, a new graduate who had started working at the same time as I did. I had an intuitive sense from the beginning that I might encounter some problems from her, as well as with another new graduate nurse who also worked full time. This premonition came true when shortly after my promotion, Nurse C said to me, "Who do you think you are? Miss Nancy Nurse? How did you get to be team leader? I work here full time, and I should be team leader, not you!" We had had a tense relationship since, and today it was coming to a head.

As I made my rounds to check on how the staff were doing, I noticed that she was not on the unit and her patients had not been seen by her. I went to look for her and asked whether anyone had seen her or talked with her, and when I couldn't find her I notified the head nurse. She informed me that the nurse refused to work for me. At first I was concerned that this would reflect badly upon me; after experiencing such a lack of support from my own mother, I expected other women to treat me the same way. Thankfully, Shirley understood the situation and took my side. I reassigned the patients to other team members, and the staff nurse was fired for abandoning the unit and her patients. I felt supported and confirmed in my professional judgement by Shirley, whom I held in high esteem.

A year after I started, the director of nursing for the medical unit called me into her office and said she had heard from Shirley that I was planning to transfer to psychiatry in a month. When I confirmed this was true, she asked me to reconsider. She told me, "You have outstanding medical skills, and we would hate to lose you."

This was an incredibly validating moment for me. I was now the person I knew I could be, one that my mom had always discouraged me from being: an excellent nurse.

## Chapter 15

### Following My Calling

The day finally arrived when I began working on the psychiatric unit as the charge nurse, with shifts going from 11:00 PM to 7:00 AM two nights a week. I was hired to be the charge nurse even though I had not worked in psychiatry before because of the high recommendation given by my former supervisors. Even though I was working the night shift, I completed my week-long hospital orientation during the day shift so I could meet all the nursing staff and become familiar with the programs the patients were expected to participate in throughout the day.

One of the reasons I wanted to leave my previous medical unit despite their asking me to stay was that I enjoyed listening to patients and allowing them to talk about their feelings around their illness and their life issues. These conversations were not possible when I was assigned to six patients who almost all needed complete help in getting bathed, changing their bed linens, and eating. Then, when I was assigned as team leader, I did not have any patients to care for directly because I was supervising the nurses and nurse aides as well as the overall patient care on my team. The physical demands on the nurses in that unit were immense, and the time to sit and talk to each patient was a luxury that none of us possessed. In contrast, a nurse working in psychiatry was *expected* to sit and engage in a conversation with her patients, and physical care was at a minimum since ninety-five percent of the patients were only there for mental health issues.

I felt a special calling to be a psychiatric nurse which partly came from personal experience. When I was ten years old, I heard my parents arguing about what the family needed to do about my maternal grandfather, who I had often heard was "crazy." He seemed to be so much fun when we visited him—he always played the guitar and sang songs with the family around the stove fireplace. However, what I didn't know when I was young was that he was also a very bitter man. When he was about nine years old, he was playing near the trolley car tracks and fell onto them. A trolley car then ran over his leg, and he ended up having half of his leg amputated. He was awarded a considerable amount of money for this loss and was supposed to receive it when he was an adult, but unfortunately this compensation never came through due to the Great Depression. After not only losing his leg but also being betrayed by the economy, he took on a very jaded view of the world. He would get into terrible arguments with my mother from time to time, and I remember one that made me very scared.

One day, when I was young, I was in the living room playing with my aunts and uncles when the sounds from the kitchen went from laughter to anger and yelling. We did not know what started this particular argument, but soon after we heard my dad say, "Put that knife down now!" Apparently, my grandfather had come after my mother in his wheelchair with a knife in his hand. We were all scared and thought he was going to kill her. Soon after the fight started, my parents ran out from the kitchen, grabbed me and Sonny, and rushed us to our car so we could leave immediately. We never talked about this event, but I realized my grandfather was not the happy man I thought he was.

The family decided to put him in a psychiatric hospital in 1952, and we went to visit him once. I remember we had to drive down this long and winding driveway, and at the end was a very large, gray brick building with black iron bars on the windows. It was both scary and intriguing. Sonny and I stayed in the car with my dad while my mother went inside, and I wondered what was happening in this foreboding building. Twenty years later, my new position would allow me to find out what was behind the locked doors.

As a psychiatric nurse, I shed my white uniform and cap like a snake shedding its skin. Wearing our street clothes helped the psychiatric patients feel more comfortable and provide the warmth that would allow for open communication. This seemed like the perfect place to learn, and to outgrow my old self. I might as well learn to value alien experiences without hiding behind the uniform. I wanted to respond with supple curiosity, not rigid fear, when a person with mental illness entered into my world. Unfortunately, I soon realized that my experience in the unit did not fully translate to the rest of my life. In the unit, I knew the patient's diagnosis, what to expect from them, and how to best treat and handle them. In the rest of the world, I wouldn't know the diagnosis of the person or what to expect from him/her, so meeting people in the everyday world was far more dangerous.

My choice to work in psychiatry was looked upon with fear and fascination by my peers. The fear existed because most people did not know much about mental illness since no one really talked about it at the time. If they did know someone with a mental illness, they usually blocked it out of their minds or denied the person was actually ill. The fascination came because they themselves could not imagine working in the unknown and uncharted field of psychiatry. In the medical, surgical, pediatric, and maternity fields, you are given specific treatments and procedures to follow that will help heal each patient. In psychiatry, however, you must rely on your own intuitive instincts and the use of your personality and people skills, along with having the ability to communicate with not only your patient but also the staff you are working with at any given time.

The psychiatric unit was located on the thirteenth floor of the same hospital I had been working at during the past year. I was looking forward to this new experience; something that was more difficult and less certain. At least, that's how I explained this decision to exile myself from the dependable source of satisfaction provided by the medical unit. As the charge nurse, I would be the only registered nurse on the psychiatric unit, with two nurse aides and twenty-five patients under my care. The diagnoses included depression, anxiety, manic depression, alcoholism, and schizophrenia, which meant I would now have to expose myself to riskier types of connection.

When I left my beautiful home in Downers Grove on a warm summer night to attend my first shift as a psychiatric nurse, I once again asked myself why I was doing this. I did not need to work, and I had achieved everything I wanted to accomplish. Why was I forcing myself to be away from my family?

As I reflect back on my life, I believe I pushed myself forward to prove to myself I could handle these challenging situations. I had spent a long time feeling poorly about myself, and I needed to prove that I deserved to live the wonderful life I was living with Patrick and Liz in our beautiful new home.

As I entered the parking lot of the hospital at 10:45 PM, I again asked why I was putting myself in this danger. The hospital was located in a high crime area, so much so that there were security guards to escort us to the hospital from the parking lot. Once I made it to the entrance, however, I decided that I was ready for this challenge. I wanted to pursue this opportunity for my own personal growth as well as for professional experience. It was only two nights a week and again only for one year. I could do this.

Walking in to my first shift, I read a sign on the desk of the head nurse that said, "In order to lead others, one must be willing to walk alone." This message resonated with me then, and it continued to resonate with me throughout my professional life journey. It reminded me that my quest to be a nurse was a solitary one that I pursued without the support of my family, and that if I wanted to become the woman and mother that I knew I could be, I needed to listen to myself and be a role model for my children as they entered into an unknown world.

# Chapter 16

## Don't Judge a Book by Its Cover

As I took out the keys to open the door to the locked psychiatric unit, I wondered what kind of night I was going to have. It had been a week since I last worked on the unit, and I was not yet familiar with the patients. This was the disadvantage of only working two nights a week; in the time in between my shifts, there could have been some patients who were discharged and new patients who were admitted.

As I entered the unit, I was always aware of the possibility of a patient wanting to escape. This unit was a locked unit, which meant that only the doctors and nurses working on the unit had access—all other medical personnel and patient visitors had to be escorted in and out. I opened the door slowly and made sure that it closed behind me.

As I walked down the hall, I made sure to stay aware of my surroundings. The nurses station was located in the center of the unit and was secured by pliable glass windows that went from the desk counters to the ceiling in an L shape. This gave the nursing and medical staff a view of the patients in the lounge and TV area as well as access to both sides of the unit where patients' rooms are located. This also served as a place to keep the staff safe if a patient became violent.

The evening charge nurse gave me and the two nurse aides the report for our twenty-five patients along with their diagnoses and any potential lab tests that must be done for the following day so we knew if they had any restrictions. For example, a patient who had to go for an early electroshock therapy treatment could not eat or drink anything except water beforehand. The report also included any potential night admissions that may occur from both the treating physician and the emergency room. As the only registered nurse on the unit, I was responsible for giving the patients any medications they may require, including emergency sedatives.

If you are a new professional nurse or medical intern, it is important to know that the current hospital staff may not support you until you prove yourself to be competent. As such, each night that I was working, I tried to get along with the people that I would be working with. I was thirty-two years old, and the two African-American nurse aides were in their early fifties with several years of tenure on the psychiatric unit. I knew I needed to prove my skills as a nurse leader, especially since I only worked two nights a week compared to their five days and had much less experience. I shared the responsibility of checking on the patients while they took their evening break and spent time listening to the patients who had trouble sleeping.

One of the first nights I worked with them, I noticed how they looked me up and down as I entered the nurses station to get the evening report. They both sat across from me with their arms crossed and said nothing after I introduced myself, acting as if they didn't hear me. I thought, *oh no, here we go again with*

*having to work with staff to whom I will need to prove myself.*
This situation was not unlike my experience when I became
team leader of the medical unit. They only saw me as the new
young charge nurse; they had no idea who I was as a person,
and I had no idea who they were outside of this psychiatric
unit. However, my nursing experience made me realize that no
matter where we are in the social structure of the hospital, we
all want to be accepted and respected for who we are as human
beings. I wanted to treat these two women with the respect
and acknowledgment of who they were—people who were
there because they needed to work to help with their family's
economic situation. I could learn from their twenty years of
psychiatric nursing experience, if I allowed myself to.

I broke the silence and asked, "Mrs. X and Y, can we set a
time tonight when it is convenient for the both of you to discuss
any of your nursing experiences with psychiatric patients that
could be helpful to me as a new nurse?" They both looked at
one another, and then agreed. We later met and discussed the
patients that were presently on the unit in depth, talking about
different strategies and which ones were the most helpful. This
discussion helped to decrease the tension that had existed
between us, and I felt there was an opening for further growth
and trust.

On a psychiatric ward, it is incredibly important to work
well with your colleagues. For example, one night a patient
very unexpectedly became out of control and started to yell
and pace up and down the halls of the unit. There was no prior
communication from the evening charge nurse that this patient
was agitated and could potentially be a problem—often there
will be behavioral changes in a patient that will give us some
warning that an outburst may happen, but this evening there
was none. Adrenaline coursed through my body, causing my

heart to race and my body to react as fast as it could to take care of the situation.

Usually I try to talk to the patient and get her to calm down, but in this instance it was impossible since she was so agitated. I had to direct each of the aides and let them know what part of the patient's body to hold to keep both the patient and themselves safe. Preventing physical injury is our primary concern. As I injected the patient with a sedative, I also talked to her and let her know she would be okay. This can be a very frightening experience for the patient as well as the nursing staff, so we need to trust one another and know what we are doing is in the best interest of the patient. We put the patient in leather restraints and placed her in a quiet room, as was the procedure, and the nursing staff checked on her every fifteen minutes to assess how she was doing. By morning, the patient was feeling much better.

Years later, I was asked to testify as a psychiatric nurse expert witness on behalf of a plaintiff's firm for a case of negligence that occurred at another prominent hospital. The situation involved a male attorney in his late thirties who was married with two young children. He had been admitted to the medical unit for abdominal pain and depression, and when there was no physical explanations for his abdominal pain he was then admitted to the psychiatric unit because of his consistent and increasing depression.

The next day, the patient's attorney came to visit. Since he was feeling so much better and his affect was good, the doctor and nursing staff said it was okay for him to go to the attorney's office to take care of some business. The patient's chart stated that he came back to the unit in a good mood.

That night the patient was found dead, hung by his bed sheets.

In my review of the medical record of this patient, I noticed there was no follow up or conversation with the patient during the evening to assess his mood. It is a well-known fact that the most important time in a depressed patient's care is when they suddenly become happy, as that is often a sign that they have decided to commit suicide. The reason he went to his attorney's office was to sign the necessary insurance papers so that his wife and young children would be taken care of. He returned to the unit a few hours later feeling in a good mood because he knew he had taken care of business, and he then decided to end his life, which he accomplished that night. The nursing staff were also negligent because they failed to make the required half hour checks on each patient, which are especially important for a patient who is very depressed.

I believe the saying that is the title of this chapter, don't judge a book by its cover, is an important message. There are so many interactions in our daily lives where we operate at such a superficial level. We cannot know all the hidden parts of another person's life or psyche as we usually reserve sharing these parts of ourselves for only a small number of intimate family members and friends. As a result, I think we tend to judge one another unconsciously based on our own personal life experiences. As a psychiatric nurse who is responsible for observing the shift of a patient's mood and demeanor, it is extremely important to look under the surface and observe and report those behaviors—it could literally save a life.

This man's death still haunts me thirty-one years later, even though it was not my fault. I still feel the real sadness of the loss of a beautiful, gifted human being who was tormented by the demons that he alone knew and struggled against. Despite being in a place designed to help him with his pain, he succumbed to his impulse to end it all. It was a tragic end to a woefully short life.

### Chapter 17

#### The Awakening

In 1973, I decided to return to school once again to obtain my bachelor's degree in nursing. This would give me more career options, such as teaching nursing, and the financial pay was higher than I would have available to me with an associate degree. This did not go over well with Ed. Instead of being happy for me, he was more and more displeased with my desire to succeed in the world, just like my mother had been. I wanted Ed to fully support me going back to school, but I made the decision to return in spite of his not wanting me to continue.

I learned in my therapy sessions that Ed was threatened by my drive to obtain my nursing degree because he was afraid of losing me. Ironically, this attitude was only pushing me away.

While I was working on the psychiatric unit two nights a week, I was also taking organic and inorganic chemistry classes in the evenings I was not working in order to fulfill my science class requirement to enter the University of Illinois. I also had already completed several of the courses for the bachelor degree when I was pursuing my associate degree, and if I could succeed in passing the tests to challenge these courses with a score of at least 75% then I could get my degree in one year instead of two. Preparing for these exams was time consuming and stressful, especially since I did most of my studying at night or the early morning while Patrick and Elizabeth were asleep. I completed these exams by the spring of 1973, and I was elated when I learned that I had passed them all. I was then accepted to start the program at the University of Illinois starting that same fall.

One of the requirements for the program was a course in biochemistry for nurses that was held in the late afternoons four times a week. I was already going to be carrying seventeen units in the first semester of my program, and adding this course meant I would get home late every day and miss spending time with my children. After doing some research, I found a college located in the suburban area where I lived and that offered a four-week intensive biochemistry class over the summer. If I was allowed to take this course instead, I could complete it before the fall semester began and spend more time with my family.

I met with the nursing faculty at the University of Illinois to see whether this course could meet the requirements of the nursing program, bringing a copy of the textbook for their approval. I was so happy and relieved when they said they would accept the course, and that because it was more difficult than the one they offered, they would accept a "D" as a passing grade. I was the only female in the class and the only non-medical student. When I received a "B" as a final grade, I cried with happiness and pride.

This course also offered an unexpected defining moment in my life. The professor called me "Lilly" during this class, and I instantly loved the name. I was named Lillian after my mother, and I had never liked that we shared the same first name. After taking this course, I knew that when the time was right I would change my name to "Lilly," and I did so in 1980.

Unfortunately, this biochemistry class started the same week that my husband Ed was to attend a very important insurance conference in Banff, Canada, and we had planned to go together as a family trip. I explained this dilemma to the professor, and thankfully he said I could just take my textbook with me and read the assignments for the week that I was away. I could hardly believe how supportive he was. I drove with Ed and my two children from Illinois to Banff, reading my biochemistry book several hours a day.

The Banff Springs Hotel was a castle-like building nestled in the Canadian Rockies that had been built in the nineteenth century. As soon as we settled into our room, eight-year-old Patrick and five-year-old Liz wanted to go out and explore the winding hallways of this mystical castle and ride the elevators with the open iron pull doors that led to more interesting places. They had a fabulous time exploring all the nooks and crannies of this historic hotel. I loved watching them laugh with glee and encourage one another to explore on their own, giving them the freedom to roam wherever they wanted every day. I studied by the pool as they swam and loved having time to hang out with them all day without having to leave for work in the evenings. The trip was magical for us, and the kids still talk about it as being one of their happiest memories of their childhood.

The evening before we left for home, Ed and I attended a cocktail party and dinner reception that was held for all two hundred of the attendees. After leaving our kids at the hotel with a sitter, Ed and I entered a large dining room with a very high vaulted ceiling and several floor-to-ceiling windows that had old-world floral drapes held back with gold ties. There were several large chandeliers providing dim lighting, and I felt as if I was entering another world. I was looking forward to a fun evening after studying all day and playing with Patrick and Elizabeth. What I did not anticipate was that I would have a very strong attraction to one of my husband's colleagues.

Ed was busy as usual during the cocktail reception making small talk with his business associates, so I was on my own trying to tap into my professional, confident self so I could be the "good wife." As I walked around the room looking for people I knew whom I could chat with, I felt someone come up behind me. It was a couple I had played tennis with earlier in the day, and they wanted to introduce me to a friend they had with them.

I turned around and immediately saw this tall, very handsome man with salt and pepper curly hair. He looked like a younger Burt Bacharach. I slowly met his piercing light blue eyes, and the sexual vibrations between us were immense. As he held my gaze and my hand, perhaps a little longer than usual, he said, "I noticed you earlier today when you were playing tennis, and you are not bad!" We laughed and started talking as the other couple disappeared back into the crowd.

We were seated at different tables across the room for the dinner, but his chair was in my direct view so the flirtation continued throughout—Ed was too busy socializing to notice what was going on. After dinner, the man stopped by my table and asked if I would like to go for a walk with him. Ed had left to meet up with some business friends for some drinks, so I agreed.

As soon as the two of us were in a private hallway we could not stop kissing one another—we were fully engaged in these sexual feelings. It was an awakening within myself that I did not feel I was capable of experiencing. My body just wanted to melt into his. We ended up in Ed and my hotel room, which was next to our children's room. Once we were in this space, I felt so guilty that I knew I had to stop this before it became more than I could handle. I put an end to what we were doing and had him leave.

The worst part came after my husband returned to our room. This male friend called soon after Ed arrived and said he wanted to meet me again the next day. Luckily, I answered the phone, but I had to talk in cryptic messages. I could hardly believe that I was in this situation. After I hung up, Ed asked who had called and I told him the truth about what had happened that evening. He was surprised and devastated, and he started to cry. Ed never cried. I knew he never expected anything like this to happen, because up until this point I was truly the "good wife."

It was very uncomfortable to wake up next to Ed the following morning. He was still upset and could not understand how I could be attracted to another man. Since we were leaving Banff that day, we decided to talk again about this situation after we were home so we had some time to reflect on what happened. These feelings I had experienced were new to me, and I was going to have to explore what they meant for me and my relationship with Ed.

On our drive back, I thought a lot about this other man and was surprised that I had allowed the flirtation to go as far as it did. Initially I felt guilty, but after a few days I was amazed at myself to be feeling this way. In retrospect, my earlier yearning for an affair was a yearning to complete myself as a person. Once I started down this road of self-exploration, I had become happy and content within myself. Now, five years after starting therapy, I had become a new woman, and as a result my relationship with my husband was slowly but persistently wearing away.

There comes a time when something powerful shows up and tells you that there is more to life than what you know and feel. As I've mentioned before, I believe that every person enters your life for a reason. This man had entered my life to be my wake-up call and show me how much I was missing. The parenting side of Ed and my relationship was always strong and formidable, but I now knew that it simply wasn't enough.

## Chapter 18

### Family Crisis

The year 1974 started off with Patrick, age ten, and Elizabeth, age seven, home with pneumonia for the entire month of January. I was beside myself with worry. Patrick came down with pneumonia first, and he was very sick. His pediatrician allowed him to stay home instead admitting him to the hospital because he felt I, being a nurse, could take care of him. Elizabeth then got pneumonia a week later. They were both on antibiotics, and we had steam flowing in their bedrooms and the family room to help with their breathing and chest congestion. I was about to enter the winter semester of my nursing program, which was also going to be full time, and my stress level and worry for my children was overwhelming. What good mother would leave her kids to pursue her career under these circumstances? I wanted to quit the nursing program, even though I was just seven months away from graduating, as I could not fathom how to handle this situation.

My therapy sessions continued during this stressful time, and after many discussions with my therapist and with Ed, we decided that I would continue with my classes and Ed would work from home to be with our children. He did it more in the interest of caring for our children than as a supportive act towards me and my goals, but I was grateful nonetheless. Thankfully, Patrick and Elizabeth—being the resilient children they were—managed to get back to their healthy selves by the end of January and went back to school.

The relationship between Ed and me had remained strained since my encounter with his colleague at the conference in Banff the previous summer. I learned in my course in family therapy that when one person in a family is hurting, all members of that family are hurting. I now believe that Patrick and Elizabeth became ill with pneumonia because the stress in our marriage caused their immune systems to become compromised, making them both susceptible to getting this virus. I felt guilty because it was my decision to pursue this degree and not be satisfied to stay at home.

In retrospect, this feeling of guilt was perhaps me being a bit harsh on myself. Back in 1969, prior to my entering the associate nursing program and before I started therapy, I just wanted to die. I was not happy being at home, and my marriage to Ed was waning. I loved being a mother to Patrick and Elizabeth with all my heart, but I did not feel good about myself without a career. It seems that I would feel guilty about whatever choice I made and the consequences that the decision would have on my children. I can now see that I did what I needed to do to be the best person and mother possible.

Around this time I met another nurse, Carol, who had been through a divorce and had two children close in age to my own. When I told her I was thinking about getting a divorce, she gave me the name of her lawyer in case I needed it. At the time, it was difficult for me to think about going through with meeting a lawyer and talking about divorce. Not only did I not have anyone in my family that was divorced, but my plate was full and my time limited. However, I felt stuck in my relationship, and I was starting to feel that I would rather die than stay married to Ed. The thought of my two children without their mother was unacceptable to me, so this pushed me to take my feelings about my marriage seriously and not just dismiss them as unimportant. I'd discussed these feelings with my psychiatrist for over two years, and he helped me come to the realization that my marriage was over.

In 1974, after eleven years of marriage, I went to see the divorce lawyer my friend Carol had recommended. The difficulty of getting a divorce at this time was that you needed to claim that there had been "mental cruelty"; there was no such thing as a "no-fault" divorce in Illinois at this time. I look back now and I can see how this law was created to make it difficult for a wife to divorce her husband. A woman needed concrete proof of mental cruelty to leave their marriage, but I do not believe that this law applied to men. There was no cruelty in our marriage—we had simply grown apart—so the lawyer recommended that we first have a year of separation before we finalized the divorce process. I had no problem with this requirement as I was in no hurry.

After paying the retainer fee and leaving his office, I asked myself, why am I made this way? Why can't I be happy with what everyone sees as the perfect relationship? There were no other parties involved, no alcohol, and no physical abuse. Ed was a good father and a good financial provider. Why was I not happy to live in this beautiful home in this upper-middle-class neighborhood with a husband who cares for me?

I did not know how to tell Ed I wanted a divorce, so I kept stalling. My hand was forced, though, when Ed came up to me a few days later as I was washing the dishes and said, "What is this check for seven hundred dollars to Mr. X?"

My stomach dropped. I turned off the water, dried my hands on the towel lying next to the sink, and gulped. I thought my heart was going to jump out of my body with the heavy pounding I felt against my chest. I could feel the sweat in my palms as I slowly turned around to face Ed, who was standing close behind me. Thankfully, the kids were outside playing and would not witness this conversation. I said, "It is a retainer for the lawyer I hired."

"What for?"

"We need to sit down and talk before the kids come in for dinner. Ed, I am going to divorce you after I finish school. You must know that I have not been happy for a long time, and there is no point in us staying in a marriage that is not working."

Ed looked at me in shock. "This is all because of the psychiatrist isn't it? I knew something would happen if you continued with your therapy. Was this his idea?"

I shook my head. "I have thought about this decision for a long time. I know this is a surprise to you, so why don't we take a break for now and think about the best time to tell the kids." I felt sick to my stomach, but I also felt relieved that this was finally out in the open. As I finished talking, my body filled with peace.

Ed was in a state of disbelief. He just sat there looking at me, then stared at the floor as he slowly got up from the kitchen table to go upstairs. He did not try and talk me out of it or admit that he was not happy either, although I have no idea if he was happy in our marriage or not as he never talked about it. As far as I could tell, he simply seemed to accept our relationship for what it was.

For the next two weeks, Ed and I maintained our usual superficial relationship. We continued to sleep in the same bed and went through the motions of being parents. Ed and I always liked one another, and so we were able to get along well for the sake of our dear children. There was no further talk about our divorce; my mind was made up a long time ago.

At the end of June 1974, when the kids were off school for the summer, I knew it was time to tell them what was happening. I sat Patrick and Liz down and told them that their dad and I would be living in different houses starting at the end of August. These were the most painful words I ever had to say in my life, and I felt sick with anxiety as I looked into their sweet and innocent faces. I was doing my best to reassure them that this decision had nothing to do with them when Patrick abruptly pushed his chair back from the table with an anger that I had not seen before and stormed off. Elizabeth sat there for a moment, and then without saying a word she got up and followed her brother to play outside with their friends.

I can never take this day away, and I know in my heart and soul that I was the cause of this painful experience for not only my two young, innocent children, but for my husband as well. But how are you supposed to know at nineteen years old that the man you choose to marry will be the one you'd want to be with forever? Ed met all the criteria to be my perfect husband, but in the end we just wanted such different things.

While I knew that many people would judge me for making this difficult decision to leave Ed, I also believed in my heart and soul I had only three people that I was accountable to: my two children and God. This decision was painful and heartbreaking, but I could only think about my patients who were on their death beds saying, "I wish I had done..."

# PART TWO

## New Beginnings

# Chapter 19

## The Separation

Ed moved out of our home in August 1974, the same day that I graduated with my bachelor degree and two months after he first learned I was divorcing him. Ed and I decided that he would stay in the house until I graduated, and then he would find his own place—it was common in divorce at this time that the children stay with the mother in the family home. He found a two-bedroom apartment in the next town over, about twenty minutes away. It was a lovely apartment complex that had a ski lift in the winter and activities for adults and children in the summer. It was an unusual place to have skiing available because we lived in flat Illinois.

My graduation was bittersweet. Elizabeth, age seven at the time, was very happy to join me. She wore a long blue dress that showed off her dark brown curly hair and was very charming when I introduced her to my classmates. I was happy to have her with me at the ceremony; I wanted her to feel proud of her mom, and to be a good role model for her.

Patrick, who was eleven, refused to come to my graduation

because he was still very angry with me. This rejection was painful for me, but I did not push him to come because I knew that my decision was the reason he was feeling this way. I was his mother, and I wanted to support him by showing him that it was okay to be angry with me. I knew that at some point in his life, he would look back and realize how much I loved him.

The graduation was a small, intimate celebration of registered nurses who had obtained their Bachelor of Science in Nursing. Liz and I walked into the small auditorium where the celebration was being held and sat in the front row with my close friends Suzanne, Diane, Ginny, and Carol. The director of nursing called each of us by name, one by one, to come up to the stage to get our hard-earned diplomas. It was a low-key event as far as celebrations are concerned, but it was a powerful and significant one for me, both personally and professionally, as well as for my nursing friends. It was the reward for a culmination of years of studying, sacrificing our time and energy and taking attention away from our families. It opened the doors to many different careers and was the beginning of a new life for me as a single mother.

There was a cocktail reception following the ceremony and Liz enjoyed spending time with me and my friends as we all laughed and felt a sense of relief and accomplishment. My happiness around graduating was mixed with the anticipation of how Elizabeth and I were going to feel when we arrived home to the reality that Ed was no longer living with us. I felt sad and had an emptiness in the pit of my stomach. I also knew that if I was feeling this way, then so did my two young children. There was no escaping the consequence of this painful experience for them, and I had to acknowledge this within my heart. I just hoped that someday they would come to understand that even though I loved them very much, I could not stay in an unhappy marriage.

Patrick came home the following afternoon after staying with his father in his new apartment, and he just stomped up to his room and slammed the door. He later came downstairs and joined Liz and me for dinner, but he sat down at the kitchen table without saying a word and stared at the floor while he ate, making it clear that he did not want to talk. I gave them both the space they needed while also making sure they understood that they were free to express their feelings about our divorce any time they wanted to.

I tried to make our home as happy as I could under the circumstances. The arrangement between Ed and me, along with our lawyers, was that I would stay in the house with Patrick and Elizabeth until they were eighteen years of age, and they were to spend their weekends with Ed. However, Ed was a good father, so we did not always stick to a strict schedule depending on the kids' school activities and interests. We tried to maintain continuity and have similar boundaries so they knew what to expect from us as parents, and so as to provide a sense of security and love.

Our families and friends were very surprised when they learned that Ed and I were separating. There were even several of Ed's friends that called me to try and change my mind about the divorce. I knew that not everyone would understand this decision as I had chosen not to discuss the intimacies of my marriage with the people around me. I also knew I was going to be judged by our family and friends as none of them had ever been divorced. I held fast though, knowing that I had made the right choice for myself.

It is a sad fact of life that we find out who our true friends are when we enter a time and place in our life that we become a threat. We all change over time, and some of our friends will change with us while others will not. Just like our romantic relationships, we either grow together in friendship or the relationship dies.

Following our separation, I stopped getting invitations to social events with other couples even though Ed was still included. It was a sad realization for me, but I was developing a new social group with my nursing colleagues so I simply focused my time and energy on those friendships. I later found out through mutual friends that the reason I was no longer included in these social events was because the women in the group had started to see me as a threat. I was so surprised and hurt to hear this. How was I a threat? I had no interest in their husbands and was not flirtatious with them. If anyone was flirtatious, it was Ed; he was the extrovert. There was also the belief among these friends that the reason I left Ed was because I met a doctor at my work. After all, why else would I leave my husband and our wonderful lifestyle?

Two years later, Paula shared with me that the true reason behind our friends' concerns was that they thought if Ed and I, the picture of an ideal couple, were getting a divorce, then it could happen to them too. The only way they were able to deal with this threat to their own relationship was to exclude me entirely. I had to step back and understand that they did not know me or my reasons for leaving since I was a private person who worked out my issues in therapy. They could only react to the reality that they saw.

Someone I grew closer to during this time was a woman named Suzanne who I met in the associate nursing program in 1969. She also lived in Downers Grove, and when we were in school we had driven to our classes together every day. Suzanne was five years older than me and had two teenage children, and her husband was also very successful. We had a lot in common and had much to share with one another. As we drove together, we would complain about the nursing instructors, our husbands, and the challenge of combining school and family. We also were both in therapy with different psychiatrists and had similar issues with our mothers. We developed a strong friendship, and she followed me to Rush Presbyterian St. Luke's Hospital where she worked in the operating room. She was inspired by my career goal of obtaining my bachelor's degree and decided to follow me, and we both graduated together in the class of 1974.

Suzanne also struggled in her marriage as she grew professionally, and she decided to pursue a divorce from her husband at the same time as I was beginning my separation. Suzanne was my confidante and continues to be a special friend in my life today.

In the fall of 1974, I started teaching at the Michael Reese School of Nursing as a psychiatric instructor with a starting salary of eleven thousand dollars a year. The school of nursing was affiliated with the University of Chicago and was located on the south side of the city, which was a forty-five-minute commute each way. The upside was that I could work from home to prepare my lectures.

I felt passionately inspired by and dedicated to my new role as a nursing instructor. I was delighted to lecture on the subjects of manic depression and suicide since I had firsthand experience with these conditions from working as a psychiatric nurse. I loved having the freedom to work at home a few hours a week so I could spend more time with my kids. I had the support and the financial backing I needed to do what I loved most: reading and having flexibility with my schedule.

Patrick and Elizabeth had now settled into a routine and were doing well in school, and they enjoyed their time with Ed on the weekends. Ed and I maintained open communication with one another regarding the kids, and the tension between us was minimal. Patrick was involved in baseball and Liz enjoyed being on a swim team. They were loved by me and their father, and I think the fact that Ed and I were strong parents helped them to adjust to our changing family dynamics. Patrick was no longer angry with me, and I think they both came to realize that they were getting the best of both their mother and father. There was much less tension between Ed and me now that we were separated than there had been when we were together. Neither of us had another person in our lives, so our priority was their happiness and welfare. I think Patrick and Liz also realized that this arrangement had certain benefits for them; they loved spending the weekends skiing with their dad and doing other fun things with him that they had not done while we were married.

As I began my teaching position, I thought back to Mrs. Henderson, who had been a nursing instructor in one of my last classes for my Bachelor of Nursing program. She was my greatest role model as a woman, mother, nurse, and teacher. She was not only tall and beautiful, with brown hair and inviting brown eyes, but she was also knowledgeable in the field of public health and was supportive to her students. She had a calm energy and possessed a confident manner that I had not experienced in all my years as a nurse. She also exemplified the type of mother I wanted to be for my children, one that I did not have myself.

I recall a time during my schooling when I had to meet with her at least once a week to go over the nursing care plan for our patients. She would sit next to me and listen to my plan for the week and gently ask questions that made me feel confident and helped me come up with solutions that I would not have thought on my own. She was the kind of person I wanted to be for my students. I had the pleasure of meeting her again after I had taken this teaching position, and she was so excited to hear about the progress of my career—being supportive, as always.

My teaching responsibilities included supervising twelve students who were at the senior level in the nursing diploma program on a psychiatric unit two days a week. As the beginning of my teaching career approached, I thought about my personal experiences with mental illness and how I might use them to help these students learn. I also thought about how overwhelming my first days on the psychiatric ward felt, perhaps due to my experience with my maternal grandfather. I decided that I would try and be aware that each one of my students would be coming to their psychiatric clinical rotation with their own personal life experiences, and so I wanted to provide each of them an opportunity to have private talks with me about their fears and concerns while on this clinical rotation.

I decided to meet with the students as a group first before we entered the psychiatric unit. I introduced myself and then asked them about their experiences with mental illness, whether they were personal or involved a family member, a friend, or some fear or attitude about psychiatric patients. We then discussed these fears and concerns as a group.

As a part of my teaching responsibilities, I wanted to establish a relationship with the head nurse of the psychiatric unit of the University of Chicago Hospital. The relationship between the nursing school and the university hospital was imperative for the nursing students to be able to obtain the clinical experience they needed to graduate, and I wanted to do everything I could to help these students succeed. The head nurse was a young African-American woman who was very compassionate and welcoming to me and the students. She had several years of experience on this unit and encouraged the students to ask the staff any questions they may have.

One of the first challenges of my teaching experience came when one of my students asked if we could talk in private after class. When we met, she revealed that she had had severe depression earlier in her life and had been admitted to this exact unit two years ago as a patient, and she was afraid that the head nurse would remember her. This situation presented a dilemma. There was a written policy in the University of Chicago's handbook for psychiatry that a patient could have no contact with the unit for four years after being discharged as a patient. It would be two more years before she met this requirement, and there was no other unit at this hospital where she could get the experience she needed. To me, this was totally unacceptable. I could hardly believe this student had gone through two and a half years of her nursing studies and had done well through all of them only to find out in her last year that she would have to wait another two years to complete her degree because she had once been a patient of this unit. I was outraged! I complimented the student on her courage and her directness, and I assured her that I would do everything I could to help her stay in the program.

With her blessing, I went off to convince not only the director of the nursing program but also the head nurse and staff of the psychiatric unit that this student could handle the boundary issues that would arise from her situation. We won the fight, and she did a stellar job as a psychiatric nursing student. This was one of the many satisfying experiences in which I was able to make a difference in another person's life, and it filled me with joy.

I enjoyed teaching my first group more than I could have ever imagined. The mornings I met my students were filled with awe. At first, they would walk to the psychiatric unit from our pre-conference classes with trepidation, wondering what kind of patients they were going to be spending time with that day and how they were going to feel about their experience. Within a few short weeks, those same students conveyed an attitude of being in control and were able to anticipate how they were going to be helping their assigned patients to work towards reaching their goal of getting healthy enough to go home. Our meetings offered them the support and confidence they needed to become more comfortable with their own abilities, and I loved watching these bright, young nurses grow. They were six months away from graduation, and I was so happy to be a part of their positive learning experience. It was not long ago that I was in their shoes, and I remembered how I felt when I was in their shoes.

The sense of self I developed as a woman and mother through this position was exciting, and my sense of self as a teacher who could make a difference was confirmed by the reaction of my students. When the semester ended in January 1975, the students surprised me with a silver necklace that was engraved with "Your First Group." They also gave me a hand-written card with their names on it that included a special message of thanks. I was touched and so grateful that I was able to see the impact I had made on these up-and-coming nurses.

# Chapter 20

## Life as a Single Mother

As a single woman and mother, the first emotions that pervaded my everyday world were ones of freedom and happiness. I no longer had to ask Ed for permission to do something or inform him of my daily plans and activities. I was so fortunate and blessed that both Patrick and Elizabeth were good kids who were continuing to do well in school. We started to laugh more together, and Patrick had come around to loving me again.

It wasn't long after Ed and I separated that I started to make an appearance back in the world of dating. During my last semester of my bachelor's degree, there was a class assignment where we were required to interview an involved community member to describe who they were and what their contributions were as role models for future generations. I was selected to interview Larry G, who was the president of a local company in Chicago. I planned to interview him about why he donated his time and money to a community organization and how it had helped the local citizens in their daily lives. After my short phone call with Larry to set up a time to meet, I knew on an intuitive level that this man was going to ask me out. I am not sure what it was about the call that made me feel this way, but I felt strongly in my psychic self that we would date. At this time, I was a thirty-two-year-old almost-separated woman, and I was both curious and excited about entering this new world.

I was looking forward to our meeting, which had been arranged to be at a coffee shop in downtown Chicago, and when I arrived I saw that Larry was already there. He was a good-looking Jewish man in his late thirties with hazel eyes, dark brown hair, and a nice smile. He was in good physical shape and was very confident in himself, and he seemed to be a happy and positive person. I was most pleased to meet this young, good-looking man for my interview. After answering my questions he asked me out for dinner, and I thought to myself, *I knew it!* He gave me his home address and phone number and told me to call at any time.

Even though I was excited by this prospect, I had to talk to my psychiatrist about what to do. I was naïve about the dating world and a bit fearful of meeting this strange man for a dinner date. In high school I would read "romance magazines," where women meeting men always seemed to end up in an ugly, seedy hotel somewhere on the dangerous side of town. The women would then end up being abused or raped or having some other horrible thing happen to them. This memory came looming into my consciousness out of nowhere and caused me to be fearful of this invitation. Also, I was technically married, and at this time Ed was still living in the house with me and our children. Wasn't this adultery?

My psychiatrist, Dr. W, was wonderful. He listened to my fears and helped me process the old memories of my teenage experiences. He encouraged me to go on the date but told me it was my decision. In the end, I decided it was time for me to know what life was like on the other side of marriage.

I drove an hour from Downers Grove to Lincoln Park to meet with Larry at his apartment. I felt both excited and nervous about having a date with a man that no one other than my psychiatrist knew I was meeting. I wondered if I was crazy for driving into the city to meet this guy I hardly knew, yet here I was doing it anyway. I suppose I just wanted to move into another part of my life. After parking the car, I took a deep breath and told myself that this was going to be a good experience.

I was fortunate to find Larry's apartment easily. The high rise was located across the street from Lake Michigan with a lovely green park just outside of the building. I was happy to see that the environment was so beautiful. I took another deep breath as I walked into the cream-colored marble foyer of the apartment complex and looked for the apartment number on the intercom. When I found it, I took a final deep breath before pushing the buzzer. Okay, here goes nothing!

Larry answered right away and buzzed me in to his twentieth-floor apartment. My anxiety increased as the elevator slowly rose up through the building, and I thought about just turning around and going home. But I knew that soon there was going to be no going back home to my familiar life as Ed's wife, so I needed to get past this fear. I reached his door and rang the doorbell; my heart was pounding, and I felt like running.

Larry opened the door and warmly welcomed me into his home. He said he was happy to see me as he led me into the most spectacular living room, with floor-to-ceiling windows that overlooked Lincoln Park with a beautiful view of Lake Michigan. His two-bedroom apartment was immaculate and tastefully furnished with modern furniture, creating a comfortable and inviting space.

After my initial tour of his apartment, we went for dinner at a casual Italian restaurant that was within walking distance. The food was delicious and the ambiance was perfect for a first date; not too romantic or too casual. Larry told me he had been divorced for a couple of years and had no children. He was the CEO of his company, and he was quite involved in several community organizations, one of which was the local Mental Health Association. I gleaned from our dinner conversation that Larry was a player as he talked about a few different women that he had been dating. I told him about my status of being married with an impending divorce and being the mother of two young children. I also told him I was looking forward to my graduation and upcoming position as an instructor of psychiatric nursing at Michael Reese School of Nursing.

Our conversation was both easy and fun. I was not looking for a man to be involved with in any intimate way, instead being simply curious as to what it was like to date again after being married to Ed for eleven years. Thankfully, there was no pressure from Larry to have sex. I was relieved and happy to learn that not all men out there were like the ones I had read about in those romance magazines.

Interestingly, Larry told me outright that I should not leave my husband. He explained that a woman in her early thirties who had two young children was not in a favorable position in the dating world. While I found his comments to reveal what he thought about women in my situation, I did not feel any defensiveness on my part. I was making this decision for myself, not to look for another man to replace Ed with. Larry exemplified the cultural and societal attitude that a woman is always looking for a man to take care of her. God forbid that a woman wants to leave a marriage on her own without having another man in the wings!

At the end of the night, I felt guilty when I entered my home and saw my children and Ed, even though I did not do anything wrong. I decided not see Larry again until I was legally separated a month later; there would be plenty of time to date in the near future.

Sadly, Larry and I were not destined to be friends for long. One day, after a few months of casual dating, he invited me to join him and another woman for a three-some, and he told me that he had taken photos of his other girlfriends that he wanted to share with me. This immediately brought up my childhood traumatic memory of finding the nude photos under my parents' bed. I could not believe it! Here was my first dating experience outside of my marriage, and it happened to be with a man who desired to have sex with more than one woman at a time and wanted to show me photos of his girlfriends. This was the deal breaker for me, and I ended what I had thought up until then was a nice relationship.

I learned from this experience to trust my intuition. I had sensed from the beginning that Larry had something about him that created fear in me. This fear was of the unknown, and of dating a man other than my husband. On the other side, Larry had something that triggered excitement in me as well—the excitement of the unknown, and how I would feel being in the presence of another man. How can we determine the difference? It is such a fine line to travel.

In retrospect, I am happy I traversed this difficult course so that I can now in my seventies know that I took the risk to explore the world of relationships and find myself as the woman I am today.

# Chapter 21

## Downtown Chicago Night Life

Jane, a colleague of mine from the Michael Reese School of Nursing, asked me to join her and some of her female friends for dinner and drinks after work one night. By this time I had been separated from Ed for three months and I knew Patrick and Elizabeth would be at his apartment for the weekend, so I thought that taking a Friday night off to join a friend in downtown Chicago would be fun.

I met Jane and her three friends for dinner at a small Greek restaurant in downtown Chicago. It was a warm November evening and the music from the restaurants and bars could be heard from the streets, creating a sense of fun and happiness. I did not drink at his time since I had become sensitive to alcohol after the birth of my daughter, but the food was superb and Jane and her friends were a lot of fun.

Once we finished dinner, we made our way to a bar to continue the evening. This was one of my first times out in the bar scene as a single woman and I felt awkward, like a teenager who was discovering for the first time that boys were now interested in her. Yes, I was thirty-two years of age, had two children, and had been married for eleven years, but I was thrown off by all of these men who seemed to give us the look of approval as we walked past them to find a booth where we could sit down and relax. I felt like a piece of meat that was going to the slaughterhouse. I could not believe I was here in this situation; this was not the life I was used to in my safe, suburban world where I had been protected by my husband.

After we shared an appetizer and drink together, the women I was with, including Jane, each went off on their own to circulate amongst the crowd. Jane had given me her home phone number to call if I needed her as she lived within ten minutes of downtown Chicago. As naïve as I was at this time, I could not imagine why I would want to call her; I had my own car and planned on going home after our evening ended.

Soon after my group separated, I noticed a man walking toward me. Ware was a tall, thin, good-looking guy in his mid-thirties with light brown hair and hazel eyes. As he introduced himself, I struggled to hear what he was saying over the loud music. I said hello and gave him my name, and he asked if was okay to go next door to talk in a quieter place. I consented immediately.

Ware led the way to a very nice, quiet restaurant that was attached to the bar and found a table where we could sit and talk. He had the physical characteristics of my paternal grandfather; he was tall, about six feet, three inches, and seemed like a gentle and sensitive man. He had a regal air about him, and I felt safe and protected with him by my side.

Once we settled in, we both shared why we were there that particular evening and what we did for a living. I learned that he was a lawyer who had gone to Yale Law School, and that he had never been married and had no children. We had a wonderful night, and we exchanged telephone numbers before we parted ways.

Ware was the epitome of what I looked for in a male partner, although that was not my intention at the time. He was handsome, kind, smart, and came from a well-to-do family. He opened doors for me as we entered restaurants and pulled out the chair for me as I sat down. I felt like I was the most special woman in the world when I was with him, and I loved this new life. We talked further about our lives and goals over lunch and had a wonderful time slowly getting to know one another.

After a month of phone calls and a few more lunch dates, I started to wonder if something was wrong. I felt very attracted to Ware, and even though I was certainly not looking for a husband, I loved the synchronicity of our relationship. However, he had never tried to kiss me or asked me out for an evening event. Then, as we were booking our next luncheon together about a month after our first meeting, Ware said he had to talk with me. *Oh no*, I thought, *he is going to tell me our friendship is over.*

When we met at our favorite downtown restaurant, I was filled with trepidation. I remained silent as we took our seats, anxiously awaiting to hear what he had to tell me. After a few moments, Ware finally said, "I enjoy my time with you and wish we had met several years ago. However, I do not think you know I am a homosexual."

I was so surprised that I could not think of any response at first. I was disappointed, and yet some part of me had known that there was something amiss. Even though I was somewhat saddened by this revelation, I still enjoyed spending time with him and we had a wonderful lunch sharing our personal relationship experiences.

After talking with my psychoanalyst later about what Ware had told me, I ended up crying for hours. To this day, I do not know why he had such an impact on me; perhaps I was more vulnerable than I believed myself to be.

Once I was able to calm down and accept Ware for who he was, the two of us were able to become very good friends. I invited him to parties with my nursing colleagues, and he invited me to meet his current roommate who he was involved with at the time. It was truly interesting and challenging for me to meet Ware's lover, yet I was ready and able to do so. As I entered Ware's beautiful and large living room with vista views of Michigan Avenue, Ted entered the room with a big smile on his model-perfect face. It was one of the most powerful and compassionate moments of my life. Seeing Ware with his lover was all I needed to understand that I was and would always be living in a different world than the two of them. What could I say? It takes life circumstances and experiences to truly be in touch with one's feelings about homosexuality, and as painful as it was for me, I felt happy for and accepting of Ware and his lover.

One evening, Ware accompanied me to a Fourth of July party hosted by my dear friend Maggie, who was a nurse I worked with. As the evening progressed, I noticed him checking out the men at the party. This was an eye-opening experience for me; I was used to competing with other women, but competing with men was a whole new ball game. This experience also helped confirm who I was as a person: a young, thirty-two-year-old, heterosexual woman with two young children who had been married for eleven years and was now looking to further define herself as a single woman. I had been opened up to new emotions and relationship experiences, and this allowed me to have a clearer picture of who I was and who I wanted to be.

## Chapter 22

### Coming Home

In February 1975, after I had completed my first six months of teaching, I received a phone call from my friend Ginny, who had attended the University of Illinois with me the previous year. She was working at Rush Presbyterian Hospital in the quality assurance program since we graduated last August, and she told me that there was currently an opening in the program which involved being a liaison for the psychiatry department. She thought I might be interested in the position since I had worked in this department before and she knew how much I loved working there. I told Ginny I was extremely interested and called Judy, the nursing director, for an interview.

I liked Judy immediately. She was a kind and professional woman of middle age, with dark brown hair and of average height. She conveyed confidence and had a strong background in nursing. She told me that if I took this position, I would be the lead person for communication between the two departments. I would also be responsible for overseeing the quality of nursing in psychiatry and offering continuing education classes. I would be the first nurse to work in this position, and she felt that my prior experience would be a benefit. I thought the interview went well and that this position was perfect for me.

After my interview with Judy, I was also interviewed by the director of psychiatric nursing and each of the head nurses from the adult and adolescent units. I was happy to see Ruby, the head nurse on the adult unit, and Jane, the director, since both were familiar to me from my prior experience as a charge nurse.

It did not take me long to make the decision to take the job. I loved teaching, but I missed the hustle and bustle of the large one-thousand-bed hospital. The hospital was also closer to home than the school was, and having the ability to spend more time with my children was important to me.

As I drove to work on my first day, I felt like I was going home. This was the place that had encouraged and recognized my growth as a nurse.

The quality assurance program was located in a separate department within the hospital, and we each had our own cubicle. We did not have to clock in on a time machine like the rest of the nursing staff and employees as we had the flexibility to come and go any time we wanted, so long as we put in our eight hours for the day. This was another benefit for me as a young mother because it gave me the flexibility to work the hours that were best for my growing children's needs.

My office space was located next to Maggi, who was the surgical nurse liaison, and across the room was my friend Ginny, who was the pediatric nurse liaison. Judy introduced me to my colleagues, and she encouraged us to actualize our vision of what we thought was important to provide quality patient care in our individual areas of nursing. We were given a lot of power by the new director of nursing, Luther Christman, who was also the dean of the new School of Nursing that was being established by Rush University. It was because of the leadership of Luther Christman that the quality assurance department was created and expanded to include the role of nursing. I was so happy to be a part of this innovative and challenging medical environment. I walked down the familiar halls of this large and impressive hospital that I entered as a novice nurse four years ago, and I felt so proud of the woman that I had become.

Maggi was a tall and striking woman in her late twenties with strawberry-blond hair and fair skin. She was married to Mark, who was a well-known ophthalmologist at the hospital. At first blush, she was a beautiful, smart, successful woman who was married to a successful doctor, had two Jaguars, and lived in a beautiful fifty-story high rise with four bedrooms right off Lake Michigan. She was regal and calm in her manner and never had anything negative to say about anyone. She was also a graduate of the Bachelor of Nursing program from the University of Illinois and was studying for her medical exams for entrance into the medical school. Maggi had no children and did not have a good relationship with her mother, but she would never talk about why they were estranged. She was an enigma and a special friend that I have stayed in contact with throughout all of these years.

Maggi was close to Jeanne, another coworker of ours who was also married to a doctor who worked at the hospital. Jeanne was a beautiful young woman in her late twenties with large brown eyes and long brown hair. She was quiet in her demeanor and sharp as a whip. Jeanne was responsible for the medical units of our quality assurance team.

Ginny was an attractive woman who was also in her late twenties with light brown hair and bright hazel eyes. She was knowledgeable in her nursing skills and married a nice, soft-spoken guy. Ginny worked in pediatrics and very much wanted to be a mother but had not had any success in this regard. She came from a professional and loving family, which came through in her positive attitude.

The four of us had our home base in our office space, but we were also very independent during the day as we attended to our individual responsibilities. However, we shared in-service nursing programs on a monthly basis, so we got to work with one another a few times a year. We enjoyed meeting for breakfast or lunch in Room 600, which was a private dining area for doctors, administrators, nursing faculty, and quality assurance staff. It was a large, beautiful room with picture windows and white linen table cloths. We were among the privileged to be a member, as opposed to many hospital staff members who had to eat in the cafeteria. We would also often meet after work for a drink in the comfortable lounge area off of the dining room so we could discuss our day. We shared a sense of commitment and quality in everything we did, both professionally and personally.

I felt fortunate to be back home with my nursing colleagues in the stimulating medical environment of the hospital. This was not the feeling of being home like being with my primary family. This was the feeling of being at home like I'd felt with my closest and most influential friends from Massapequa High School. These new friends seemed to have a similar quality to the high school friends that I missed seeing over the years.

I was fully engaged during the next two years in this position, but I also started taking classes towards my master's degree in psychiatric nursing two nights a week at a college near my home in Downers Grove soon after I completed my bachelor's degree. I wanted to pursue nursing because I knew from my prior experience at the Michael Reese School of Nursing that I wanted to continue to teach nursing students, a position that required a master's degree, and I also wanted to keep my options open to other jobs that would become available. Judy was in full support of me obtaining my master's degree even though it was going to eliminate me from my current position—it was the hospital policy at the time that anyone who obtained their master's degree could become a member of the teaching faculty.

In 1976, a year and a half after I had started this position, Judy, along with the director of psychiatric nursing, asked me to join them for lunch. This was unusual—I had not heard of any such meeting before. I was anxious to know what was happening. Did I do something wrong?

After my meetings with the nurses on the unit, I walked over to Room 600. I spotted the both of them at a table near the window and anxiously sat down to join them. Judy quickly spoke up to relieve the tension. "We will not keep you in suspense since we know you must be wondering what this meeting is about. We have decided to assist you in your goal of obtaining your master's degree by offering you a position where you would work twenty hours a week on a research project but get paid full time with health benefits. The research project is to develop criteria for patient care and assess how much time it took for the nurses to accomplish these criteria, which is necessary to provide quality care. The outcome of this study will be used to justify the need for a certain number of nurses to provide safe patient care. What do you think?"

I was in disbelief and felt like running out and shouting for joy! Yes, I would take them up on this extraordinary offer. The research position was the perfect job for me, and I enjoyed the challenge offered by this experience.

On top of this research position, I applied for a six-month internship in an outpatient setting as part of my clinical experience for my master's degree. I decided to expand my psychiatric education from working in an inpatient setting to an outpatient experience since there was a potential job opening once I completed my degree which would be difficult to obtain. I wanted to take every step I could to give myself the best possible chance of getting this position.

I interviewed with the director of the drug and alcohol program, who was a psychologist. He said, "We do not get nurses applying for these positions, and we usually hire psychologists for this internship. However, I notice that you have worked in a psychiatric hospital setting and your references are very good. I think that your experience and references are a plus for you, and I am going to take a chance on accepting your application. You will be in an outpatient community center for twenty hours a week, with supervision from a clinical psychologist."

The internship was everything I had hoped it would be. I enjoyed the clients I had assigned to me, which were primarily adolescents, since I did not have experience working with this group of patients. I was their therapist during my time there, and I was to listen to them and guide them in addressing their addiction issues. The frustrating part was that while I observed progress with these patients, I was not able to fully help them work through their issues during such a short period of time.

In August 1977, I graduated with my Master of Psychiatric Nursing from Rush University. I was proud of myself for sticking with this dream and seeing it through to this point, even though I faced doubts from my family. I thought back to my mother telling me not to bother with nursing school, and I could only feel glad that I proved her wrong.

## Chapter 23

### Free Spirit

One of the first purchases I bought after my divorce was finalized in August 1975 was a Triumph—no pun intended. This little brown Spitfire was just the car I wanted at the age of thirty-three. It was a two-seater convertible with a tan leather interior, which was the perfect color for me. It had space in the back for my eight-year-old daughter, Elizabeth, and a passenger seat for my eleven-year-old son Patrick.

I will always be grateful that Ed was such an excellent father, and that he and I could remain flexible in our parental arrangements. One example of this flexibility was when Ed came to stay in my home with the children for a week while I attended a nursing convention in Atlantic City, New Jersey, in 1976. I had been involved in the Illinois Nurses Association since 1971, and I wanted to attend the American Nurses Association at the national level. I was fortunate that Ed was willing to help me make this trip possible.

It was a beautiful sunny day when I set off on this new adventure as a young, single professional mother, and the anxiety and excitement I felt about driving to New Jersey on my own was exhilarating. I did not know anyone else that was planning to go to this convention, so it was just me and my new car taking off for a long drive. I had never gone on a trip by myself in my life! As I was driving off, Ed and the kids were standing outside of the home and waving goodbye to me. I smiled back at them with confidence, keeping my anxiety to myself.

I loved letting my thoughts roam free as I drove in my new car. With the convertible top down, the wind rushed past my body and I felt the warm sun on my face as I lifted it up to the sky and thanked God for everything I had at this time in my life. I had never felt more alive. Life was good, and I had so much to look forward to on this trip.

As I made my way to New Jersey, I stopped by to see my parents and my brother Guy, and spent the weekend with them. It was a warm and quick visit since my time was limited. My parents may not have been the best support when it came to my dream of becoming a nurse, but they never interfered with my decision to divorce Ed, as much as they loved him. They supported me in doing what was right for me, something that I very much appreciated.

I know they were both ultimately proud of me for obtaining my nursing degree, but I had a hard time forgetting how my mother was not there for me when I needed her most. I found over the years that I preferred my visits with her to be limited; it was my way of dealing with my underlying anger around how hard I had to struggle back then without her support. However, I wanted Patrick and Elizabeth to have their own relationship with their grandparents, so I continued to work on forgiving her. During my visit, we had a pleasant day hanging out in the back yard and sharing a delicious dinner together, and I was able to catch both of them up on what was happening with Ed, Patrick, and Elizabeth.

I also had plans to see Pat and Jerry, Ed's brother and sister-in-law, in New Jersey. Pat's short blonde hair was the same as it was when I first met her, and her blue eyes revealed a sparkle that made you feel good and always conveyed a warm welcome. When I first met her, I had been so insecure around her because I had not completed my nursing degree while she had. Now, I was her equal. We sat in her beautiful backyard among the many trees on their property and had a delightful afternoon together as two women who both chose nursing as our career and had married two brothers. Pat was no longer practicing nursing and was instead teaching biology to high school students. She and Jerry had three children—Karen, Tara, and Jerry—who were close in age to Patrick and Liz.

Jerry sat across from me at dinner, and as always, I enjoyed his company. I was so grateful that they remained open to having a relationship with me after I left Ed. Pat and Jerry were Patrick and Liz's godparents, and I wanted to continue our relationship. I was so glad that they felt the same way.

Unfortunately, Jerry died in 2008, and around this same time Pat was diagnosed with breast cancer. Pat is fine and healthy today, and although she now lives in Florida we still keep in touch through Facebook. In the summer of 2017, Pat and I arranged to have our adult children and grandchildren meet for a wonderful family reunion dinner in New York City.

A few days after my visit with Pat and Jerry, I checked into my hotel in Atlantic City, New Jersey, where the convention was being held. Once I was settled in, I took some time to just relax. I enjoyed a walk on the boardwalk and inhaled the smell of the ocean. There is nothing more delightful than the feel and smell of salt water to make you feel cleansed and alive, no matter where you come from. It was so refreshing to my soul.

I was looking forward to the convention, which included nurses from all over the United States, and the speakers were as varied as the participants. There were lectures on various nursing disciplines—including psychiatric, medical, surgical, pediatric, and obstetrical nursing—and I could move from one lecture to another and visit the booths of the exhibitors who were demonstrating their medical products and talking about their services. I felt proud of myself for being a professional nurse at this event, and I also felt a sense of disbelief that I was actually there under my own merit.

When it was time to begin the long drive back home, I settled into my car and listened to my favorite jazz music. I was happy that I had obtained this sense of accomplishment, and I felt at peace with myself in knowing that my family was not judging me for divorcing Ed. This attitude may not have been the same for all of Ed's family, but it was wonderful to at least have Pat and Jerry's acceptance.

As I continued driving and reflecting back on my life, I noticed another dark blue Triumph Spitfire passing me as I entered beautiful Pennsylvania. I could not help but smile; I found this coincidence to be rather amusing since I had not seen any other cars like mine during my entire drive to the convention. The top was down, and I could see that the driver was a cute man with reddish-brown hair. He waved as he passed me, and I noticed that he was driving alone. I figured that he would be exiting soon and that this was just a fun hello to add to my trip, so I waved back and then turned my attention elsewhere.

A few hours passed, and we were both still on the highway together. Around lunch time, he signaled me to turn off at the next exit with him. A part of me said, are you crazy? What are you doing? But another part of me said hey, why not? It would be fun to see who this guy is.

When we stepped out of our cars, I was pleasantly surprised to see a tall, nice-looking, slender young man come walking towards me. I thought, *oh my, wait until he finds out that I am this thirty-three-year-old, recently divorced, mother of two children.* We both smiled and said hello to one another. He was heading to California, and we calculated that we were going to be on the road together for another two days. Since we were driving in the same direction, we decided to have lunch and get to know each other better.

Jim was twenty-eight years old, and he lived in New York City and had never been married. He worked in finance and was on a month-long vacation to see relatives in San Francisco. In turn, I shared with him some of my story and where I was at in my life. Even though I had always been drawn towards older men, I found Jim to be a fun and attractive person.

As we both got back into our cars and started driving down the highway, I became aware of the benefit of having Jim looking out for me on this long drive back to Illinois. We continued to drive and pass one another in our respective Triumphs the rest of the day as we made our way through the state of Pennsylvania. Jim and I would signal to one another when we found a place we wanted to stop, have dinner, and sleep.

At the end of our second day, Jim and I met for dinner and further talked about our lives. It was a very relaxed and enjoyable time. I did not drink, and neither did Jim.

I surprised myself when I accepted Jim's invitation to sleep together that night. It seemed so natural, and I must admit that I felt no fear. This was a wonderful adventure on my part, and I still have no regrets to this day. He was kind, sweet, and very respectful. We shared breakfast the next morning and talked about meeting again in the next year at some designated place and exchanged home phone numbers—there were no emails or iPhones yet! Jim and I drove the rest of the day together until I had to take the exit to Chicago, Illinois. I felt sad to say goodbye to him—someone I'd met as a result of my adventure as a free spirit.

I realize now that my solo trip taught me more about myself as a woman as well as a nurse. I never imagined that I could take a long road trip by myself and spontaneously meet and spend a night with a complete stranger.

Jim and I did indeed keep in touch with one another, and in 1976 we decided to meet in Asheville, North Carolina, for a four-day weekend. At the time, I was still single and very much involved in my master's degree in psychiatric nursing, and I thought this would be another great adventure and a nice break from everyday life. What I did not realize was how conservative Asheville was.

I arrived at the Asheville airport and took a taxi to the hotel Jim had selected. I was anxious to see him again after a year apart, though we had talked frequently on the phone. I was nervous as I walked into the small boutique hotel to see my young friend from a year ago. We were supposed to be checking in as Mr. and Mrs. J, so I tried to pretend I was meeting my husband at the hotel. All was okay until I got into the room and decided to call my children to tell them that their mom had arrived safe and sound. What I did not realize was the hotel telephone operator was the same as the operator that outplaced calls. Soon after, I got a call in the room saying that I was not the wife of the person making the reservation, and we had to vacate the hotel! I had never felt so small in my life.

Jim and I had to scramble for another hotel that night.

We did have a fun experience once we found a new place, but I felt so humiliated after being told to leave. I felt judged and as if they viewed me as a criminal. Jim was surprised at their attitude toward us, but being the warm, caring man that he was, he tried to make light of the situation and managed to get me laughing about it. We ended up going on a ten-mile hike in the mountains nearby and had an incredible day together.

Six months later, Jim and I understood that our relationship was over. He found someone he loved and was going to get married, and I was ready to move on and continue my career in nursing at the graduate level. However, meeting Jim created a beautiful connection between me and my new sense of being a free spirit, and our time together has become a wonderful memory.

# Chapter 24

## My Ideal Psychiatric Nursing Position

My next career change came in 1977, when I worked and taught on a surgical unit. My former supervisors had created this position for me to use my psychiatric nurse skills in order to support the patients who had been diagnosed with cancer and their families, as well as the nursing staff, to deal with emotional turmoil that came from patients who were dying.

I had completed my master's degree in psychiatric nursing in June of that year before being offered this position as a psychiatric nursing instructor for the bachelor's degree program at the Rush University School of Nursing. This was a dream job for me. I was one of two psychiatric nurses to be selected as a faculty member at Rush University, the other one being a woman named Karen. She was a young married woman in her late twenties who had moved from Boston to Illinois with her husband specifically to accept this position. She also had recently obtained her master's degree and was looking forward to working in this new position. She was a petite woman with blond hair and blue eyes and a smile that would warm anybody's heart. She was five years my junior, and we bonded immediately. Our position included not only teaching but also carrying our own patient responsibilities on the medical and surgical units, and I loved that there was no clearly defined role.

One of the requirements for this position was for me to meet with the medical director of oncology for an interview, and then to have a separate interview with the head nurse of the surgical oncology unit. Because this position was new at the hospital and I would be interacting on a personal level with the head nurse and physicians on the unit, they had the final word on my application. This was the first time I had to meet with a physician for a job interview, and I wasn't sure what to expect.

On the day of my interview with Dr. John, I decided to wear my black suit with a white silk shirt and black heels. I liked to dress conservatively, and this skirt and jacket helped me feel both professional and comfortable. My dark brown hair was cut to shoulder length and had a wave to it, and it was often pulled back to stay out of my face. Today, though, I decided to wear it down.

The surgical oncology unit was located on the eighth floor of the hospital. As I walked down the hall, I noticed some patients in their beds with IV's and oxygen masks. There were nurses, interns, and resident doctors walking around me with a sense of purpose and direction. At the end of the hall was the nurses station, which was bustling with activity, and family members were hanging around waiting to talk with the nurse and doctor. I pictured myself as being a part of this challenging setting, and I thought that this place could possibly be my new professional home.

Finally, I saw the sign for Dr. John's office. My heart began to run faster than I expected, and the palms of my hands became sweaty. The door was open, so I looked inside to see if he was there. All of a sudden, I felt a figure rush up from behind me and say, "Hi, are you Lilly Phelan?"

I turned around to greet the figure, who introduced himself as Dr. John. He extended his hand toward me and asked me to sit down as he closed the door behind him. He was a young, handsome, five-foot-nine man with curly black hair, brown eyes, and olive skin. He was close to my age and seemed to have a good sense of humor, which can be important when working in this sort of environment. We talked about the difficulty of working with patients with cancer and the need for someone with my psychiatric background to assist him with the emotional care. Many of his patients were seriously ill, and their outcomes after surgery and chemotherapy were not always positive. He asked some questions as to what I would say to his patients or their family members under certain situations, and he seemed to be happy with my responses.

The last interview before I officially was offered the job was with the head nurse of the oncology unit, Helen. She discussed the problem of the young nurses on the unit who had to deal with the lack of emotional support for the patients that were dying of cancer. Many of the patients were young, and the medical decisions that were made went against their own personal beliefs and values. They needed someone like me on the unit to not only provide emotional support to patients and their families, but to also give emotional support to the nurses to help them cope with this emotionally draining work. I would also be responsible for teaching eight nursing students the principles of psychiatric nursing on a surgical unit.

The two interviews must have gone well, because I was accepted to the position a day later. I was elated and ready to start work, and I looked forward to creating a vision of myself in this new and exciting position.

As a psychiatric nurse teacher and consultant, I wore my street clothes, which often made patients and families feel more comfortable talking to me. I also wore a white lab coat and carried a pager so I was accessible not only to my students, but also to the nursing staff for consultations.

This position was one of the most satisfying jobs of my entire career. When a patient needed emotional support that was beyond the nurses' scope of expertise and time commitment, they would page me to come and see this patient for an assessment. I would meet and talk with the patient to discover how much of my time was needed to meet their emotional needs and then make an appointment to see them within a day or two.

For example, I was paged one day to talk with a young woman in her late thirties who had been diagnosed with ovarian cancer. She had a teenage son and a husband who rarely came to visit with her. The nursing staff had a very hard time accepting that this woman was dying of cancer at this early age, so I was called in to help both the patient and the nursing staff.

My first assessment was meeting with the patient to understand how she felt about dying. After introducing myself to her, I sat down in a chair next to her bed and listened to her fears and concerns. She seemed to feel safe and free to talk and told me that she knew her husband was having an affair. She felt sad, hurt, and alone. Unfortunately, I saw this scenario over and over again. I later discovered that this was not an unusual reaction for husbands to have when they learned that their wives were dying. In my opinion, men at this time were not taught to be independent, so when their wives were about to die they were programmed to find a replacement. Their fear of abandonment made them ensure that they would never be alone.

I found that working with cancer patients could be sad and emotionally demanding depending on the patient and the needs of the nursing staff, but I also found it to be very satisfying because they would tell me they felt better after I spent time listening to them and giving them space to share their concerns and fears with me.

My way of dealing with the intense emotions that came with this position was to work out at the gym several nights a week after work. It gave me the chance to get rid of my stress so I could fully relax at home in the evenings with Patrick and Liz.

In my year and a half of working on the oncology unit, I observed that many of the women who were receiving treatment there were the most thankful and pleasant patients I had ever met. If there was a delay in a request they had made due to other medical priorities, the patients were always gracious in forgiving the staff for being so busy and said they did not want to be a bother. They seemed so thankful for everything the nurses or doctors did to take care of them.

When I was talking with these women, I sensed that they were the soul bearers of their family. They were the one to be there for everyone during difficult times, but when they themselves became ill, their family members could not handle it and did not visit. If these family members did come to see them, they would keep the conversations superficial and say things like "Hey, you are looking great!" or "Now keep positive, you have the best doctor and he will take care of you." They were unable to honestly talk about their fears and concerns around their loved one dying. I felt sad for the patients and their families because openly discussing dying was not yet encouraged at this time in our society. This was where I came in: I provided an outlet for the patients, their family, and the nursing staff by encouraging them to talk with me about their questions and concerns.

My responsibility for providing students with learning experiences on this surgical unit was accomplished by having the students see a patient that was depressed because of their cancer diagnosis or experiencing anxiety before undergoing a surgical procedure. Many patients will have these symptoms, which are to be expected under these circumstances, and my responsibility was to teach the students what was normal or abnormal behavior.

I remember one patient in the unit who was also diagnosed with schizophrenia. I used this patient as an example to teach students that while a patient may come into the hospital with a physical illness, there may also be an underlying mental illness that nurses should learn how to recognize. Life is not always tied up in a neat bow.

When I first started this position, I was only referred to patients by Dr. John. However, I soon caught the eye of another doctor in the unit, Dr. M. He was the attending physician for urology on this same unit and dealt with men who had prostate cancer. He was a very handsome man, about forty years old, with salt and pepper hair and an intimidating manner. I had noticed him before on the unit and found him to be difficult to approach and gruff in his manner with the resident doctors. He walked down the halls of the unit with the stereotypical male swagger, the tails of his white lab coat swaying behind him. One day, he sat down next to me at the nurses station and asked what it was that I did. I was caught off guard as I didn't know why he hadn't been informed of my position already, but I answered him the best I could. After I explained what I did for Dr. John's patients, Dr. M simply said "okay" and smiled before walking away. Soon after, Dr. M began to refer me to his patients as well.

A few weeks after our meeting at the nurses station, Dr. M left me a note in my mailbox that said, "You are a beautiful woman, and I would like you to call me." I was flattered because he was a well-respected physician, but I was also distressed because Dr. M was married. I did make the call, but after he invited me out for a drink I told him I was not interested in going out with a married man. He was respectful of my response and continued to refer his patients to me.

After six months of working with Dr. John, he asked me out to dinner. I was attracted to him, but I was also apprehensive. I had noticed that many nurses were interested in Dr. John, and I knew I needed to be careful about dating someone from work. I enjoyed my position and did not want to jeopardize our fun working relationship. In the end, I decided to go on the date and just see how everything went.

This experience made me think back to everything my mother had said to me. She had told me that no doctor would ever be interested in me once they knew who I was. Well, I was now about to go on a date with a doctor, and I had been asked out by a second one. I was thankful for the years of therapy that allowed me to put these painful words in perspective and prevent these beliefs from influencing my life. I could now recognize that my mother was just doing her best to protect me based on her own personal relationships with men.

John and I met in downtown Chicago at an Italian restaurant that I had not been to before, and we had a wonderful evening together. He invited me to stay the night with him, and I was very happy and willing to know him even better.

# Chapter 25

## My Personal and Professional Life

After our first date, my relationship with John developed into a very comfortable and respectful regard toward one another. I was concerned about dating someone from work and did not want to jeopardize my professional position or get too emotionally involved with anyone, so we both decided that the best way to handle this was to keep our relationship private. It was fun to see him at work, and he would often look at me with a gleam in his eyes as we made our morning rounds together.

Over the next year in my position, I noticed a line of questioning that came up frequently with female patients who were having surgeries such as hysterectomies and mastectomies and male patients who had prostate cancer. These patients frequently expressed concerns about their personal and sexual identity after surgery, as well as their sex life. It was a topic that was uncomfortable not only for the patient but also for the nurses, who had limited knowledge on the topic and limited time to spend discussing these concerns.

I discovered that there was a new program being offered by

Loyola University on sexual dysfunction for therapists, and I thought this program would provide me with the information and guidance I needed to be able to help my patients and the nurses who were working with them. The surgical nursing department approved me to take this course and paid for me to obtain a certificate to become a sex therapist. In return, I would offer a class on human sexuality for nursing students in the Bachelor of Nursing program.

The course at Loyola was a six-week intensive, and I was assigned a male partner who was a physician. The two of us were responsible for working with a young married couple who came to the hospital clinic to get help with their sexual relationship issues. I worked with the wife in a private room while my partner worked with the husband in another. We had a list of questions which were provided to us by the clinic that were intended to help the couple get in touch with their own feelings about sex, and as we helped the couple through this process my partner and I became aware of our own feelings and attitudes.

One of the many questions was to explain how they learned about sex and from whom. How did they feel about it, and what were their experiences with it in later relationships? What did they like or not like about sex? This was a topic that I myself had issues around for a long time, but I had worked out a lot of these issues in therapy over the past eight years. By this time, I was very comfortable discussing the topic with other professionals and patients. However, I realized through this process and opportunity that I was not alone in my feelings about sex.

One of the most powerful and interesting exercises we performed was to have each spouse individually come with us into a darkened room with a full-length mirror. They were to stand naked in front of the mirror, which had a small light attached so they could see themselves, and just focus on their body. This was a wonderful way for the person to be able to look at themselves and be aware of the messages they were saying about their own body. This exercise gave each spouse important information about themselves because their self-assessment and judgments, both positive and negative, follow them into the bedroom.

Another exercise that made a significant impact was one that the couple would do at home. For the next week, they were not to touch one another sexually. Then, for the week after that, they were requested to touch one another without having intercourse. The focus was for them to discover what felt good and what did not feel good on a sensual level.

After completing the program, the couple later informed the clinic that they were now satisfied with their sexual relationship and marriage. The treatment was a success.

An exercise we did as a class in the beginning of the program involved watching three pornographic films simultaneously. One of the films depicted a loving man and woman, the second showed a homosexual relationship, and the third a lesbian relationship. We were asked to be in touch with our feelings and attitudes about the people featured in each of the films. I learned I was not as judgmental as I thought—perhaps due to my friendship with Ware. Love is love, no matter what kind of relationship you are in.

They later showed films in each of the above categories that were purely sexual in nature as opposed to the loving relationships we had previously seen. Again, we were to discuss and be aware of our feelings about these films and be in touch with our own attitude and bias toward them—there was no right or wrong attitude or answer. I realized that I did not like the purely sexual films because they seemed so cold and animalistic. I think we each came away from the seminar feeling less judgmental about an individual's sexual orientation and more open and accepting of our own personal preferences.

The most significant and comforting belief I hold to this day in my life is that there is your way and there is my way, but there is no *the* way. To me, this means that all relationships must involve open communication with one another, and that each person needs to be willing to compromise. Every couple needs to know what is important to themselves and to the other person in order to have a satisfactory partnership. This experience was a healing one for me because it helped me to understand what I did not know when I found those nude photos at ten years old.

My experience with this program was invaluable to me, both professionally and personally. I presented several seminars to nurses for continuing education, one being "Still a Taboo: Sexuality and the Nursing Process; Practical Applications." Other lectures presented to the surgical nursing staff were "Sexuality and the Patient with an Ileal-Conduit and Colostomy," "Teaching Approaches for Patients with Problems of Sexual Dysfunction," and "Educational Needs of the Oncology Patient and His/Her Family."

Through my studies and through teaching these classes, I gained some more insight into my own feelings about myself as a woman, and I was happy to see that I had grown more accepting and less critical of myself. I had received many positive comments about my looks for many years, but I did not see myself as others saw me. I always felt I could be thinner, smarter, and a better wife, mother, daughter, or friend. Now, I was slowly beginning to accept the woman I had become.

On top of my role in helping patients and their families

cope with death, I was also a member of the psychiatric liaison team. Our team consisted of four physicians as well as Karen and me. We met twice a week to go on rounds on the medical and surgical units together, identifying patients that needed psychological support. We would stop by the patient's bedside and the attending physician would introduce us. Then we would ask the patient questions about how they were feeling and if they would like a nurse to come talk to them. If a patient was severely depressed, the team would decide whether the patient should be transferred to psychiatry so they could receive more intensive care and be under closer watch for any suicidal thoughts or attempts.

One of the psychiatrists on this team was Phil E, whom I had first met when I worked in psychiatry as a staff nurse in 1971. At that time, we would often see one another in passing in the elevator; I would be leaving after my night shift at the same time he was coming in to work. He was always a person of interest for me because we always seemed to keep running into one another, yet I knew very little about him.

One day, when I was about to have lunch in the doctors dining room, I saw Phil as I was looking for a seat and I was surprised to see him motion for me to come and sit with him. He was a young Jewish man with dark hair and brown eyes and a well-trimmed beard. He was about five feet, nine inches, just a few inches taller than me, and he always seemed polite and kind in the few brief moments I had seen him on the psychiatric unit. We had first met when I was recently divorced and he had just gotten married, so today one of the first things he told me was that he was now divorced too. We both laughed and said how fun it would be to work together again on the psychiatric liaison team.

Dr. John and I continued to see one another on occasion; I

always enjoyed my time with him, and we were becoming good friends. I had previously kept my children and home off limits to anyone I was dating, but I decided to invite John over. It was now two years after my divorce, and while I was still very anxious about inviting anyone to my home, I felt that it was time to take this next step. Patrick was thirteen years old and had no interest in meeting John, but ten-year-old Elizabeth was open and ready to meet the man Mom had been talking about.

When I saw John's small red Spider convertible enter my driveway, I took a deep breath, opened the front door, and said, "Welcome to the world of suburbia." He complimented the home as I showed him around the main floor, which made me smile. Soon after, Elizabeth came running in from outside to say hello with a big smile on her face. After I introduced her to John, she said, "Okay, it was nice to meet you. I have to go back to my friend's house." We both laughed and said, "Okay, see you later."

It was mid-afternoon by this time and the sun was shining brightly through the large kitchen windows onto the dark wood cabinets, adding a sense of warmth and coziness to the room. We walked back into the living room to sit down on the olive-green velvet sofa and have a glass of wine. It was fun to have him there, but I was glad that our time was limited that day. I felt awkward and a bit disconcerted in seeing John outside of his usual element, and he seemed out of place there. It appeared that the fantasy of sharing my world with him differed from the reality of how I was feeling.

A few days later, John said to me, "You know, your house does not seem to fit you." I did not ask him what he meant by his comment as I sensed I knew the answer. He saw me to be more of a city girl, not one living in the suburbs. I sensed a shift in my feelings for John on this day, but I could not fully understand what had happened. In looking back, I think that having my personal and professional life collide in this way caused a disconnect within myself. John and I continued to date on occasion, and he remained a part of my life for several years before we went our separate ways, but our relationship was never quite the same after that day.

# Chapter 26

## It's Complicated

My life decisions have often surprised me, my family, and my friends. How can we ever fully understand why we do what we do in our lives? Do we fully comprehend the irreversible consequences of those decisions?

I achieved a huge amount of personal satisfaction after obtaining my position as a practitioner teacher. It allowed me to use my personal and professional psychiatric education to work with patients dealing with death, teach nursing students, support nursing staff, and give continuing education seminars to nurses. I met interesting and encouraging colleagues that supported my growth as a nurse. I had achieved every goal in my career as a nurse, so why, at age thirty-eight, was I now leaving nursing to pursue law school?

Perhaps the best explanation starts with my first time stepping out into the single world in 1974. One of the first lawyers I met was Ware, the handsome gentleman who had turned out to be a homosexual. During the ensuing years, I met and dated several other lawyers. They were interesting men who were fun to talk with because they were self-assured and seemed to be interested in the world around them. The common bond between them was that each one asked me, "Have you ever considered going to law school?" I felt as though I had a big neon sign on my head that said, "Guilty!"

I always immediately dismissed this question with, "Are you kidding me? I have two children and a very busy position in nursing. No way."

I had always thought of lawyers as being very smart and believed that it was primarily a man's profession. However, as I got to know each of these men, I decided that they weren't so smart after all. And, as this question kept coming up over the next year, I decided to think more about this idea while keeping an open mind.

One day, on my way home from work, I had this "AHA!" moment when I decided that I was going to apply to law school. It was late afternoon, and the sun was shining as I was heading home from Chicago. As I was driving I thought about my neighbor, Mary Ellen, who was married to a dentist and was a full-time student with four children. I thought that if she could do this, so could I.

In retrospect, my decision to go to law school was a combination of the influences of the men I met who encouraged me to pursue law and the fact that I was getting burned out from my current position. In spite of continuing my psychotherapy analysis and going to the gym to rid myself of the physical and emotional stress that came from my work, I found myself being very cynical of my suburban housewife friends who were, in my mind, living superficial lives, based on the small talk and gossip that arose when we met together. I was working with patients who were dying, and I was becoming acutely aware of how short our lives can be. The pain I saw every day was overwhelming. I will always remember a young woman I saw who was dying of ovarian cancer; no matter what medication she was given, she was still in pain. I realized that this could be me someday, and I asked myself, is this all there is? It was due to this experience and my cynical attitude that I came to believe that it was time for me to think about seeking law as another long-term profession. I wanted to work as a patient advocate, representing the rights of the mentally ill.

Since 1969, my life decisions had always involved the guidance of psychotherapy. However, my decision to look for an apartment in downtown Chicago in 1978 was made on my own. I felt this was the right direction for me, and I was both excited and frightened at the same time.

I was fortunate to find a beautiful, brand new one-bedroom apartment on the fiftieth floor of a building off Michigan Avenue, located just behind the Wrigley Building and across from the Chicago Tribune. The apartment had views of Lake Michigan and the Chicago River, and there was a new grocery store and a cleaning service on the ground floor of the building. And, to top it all off, it was a ten-minute drive to Rush University or to the University of Illinois. It was a magnificent location, and the thought of having my own place for the first time in my life was thrilling. Unfortunately, this meant leaving my fourteen-year-old son and eleven-year-old daughter as well as our beautiful four-bedroom home.

During the four years after our divorce, Ed and I tried to keep the children stable by having him stay with them at the house whenever I went out. Once I found this apartment, I suggested to Ed that he move back into the house and he was all for it. Patrick was very happy with this change; as much as he loved me, he was especially close to his dad. Elizabeth also seemed happy to have her dad at home, but I knew she was upset that I was moving, even though she did not express this to me.

Once I got settled in and started having Patrick and Elizabeth visit me, they appeared to enjoy the new living arrangements. There was a pool in the building I lived in as well as many places of interest for them to see nearby, including the Art Institute of Chicago, the Museum of Science and Industry, and the Shubert Theatre. We would go to brunch every Sunday at the Hyatt Hotel, located two blocks away, each time they visited. When Patrick and Liz had other plans on the weekends, I would drive to Downers Grove on a weekday so that we could have dinner at the Omega Restaurant.

While my personal life was going great, my transition into law school did not go as smoothly as I had planned. I had applied to two schools in Chicago and had taken the LSAT, which is an entrance exam that evaluates each student's ability to succeed in law. Unfortunately, I did not do well on the exam, but my successful nursing career and my bachelor's and master's degrees helped override the low LSAT score, along with the fact that I had been elected into the Sigma Theta Tau International Honor Society of Nursing.

In the summer of 1979, I was accepted into John Marshall Law School on a conditional basis and was required to take the contracts and torts classes, both of which are first-year classes. If I did well in these two classes, I would then be eligible for full acceptance into the night program in the fall. The program was an intense month-long commitment of four hours a day while I was still maintaining my full-time job—it was a very challenging time, but I was confident that I could succeed.

As I entered John Marshall Law School on my first day of classes, I was excited to be joining this new world. The entrance to the school was surrounded by dark wood paneling, and I was intimidated by the feeling of power that seemed to prevail in the atmosphere around me. Students were bustling all around in the halls, carrying their intimidating law books. I made my way to the classroom where we were to meet the other students and register for our classes, and while I stood in line I started a conversation with the woman in front of me. This would be the beginning of a long friendship with Cathy McCrae, a woman eight years younger than I with shoulder-length blond hair and friendly blue eyes. She had a master's degree in education but was ready to have a new career in law. She had the same conditional acceptance that I did and was hoping to get full acceptance in the fall. We went to dinner to share our hopes and dreams of starting a new career, and we had a lot of laughs together over our meal.

I loved being in the law classes and was impressed by the professors, who were friendly and wanted to see us succeed. Our torts professor, Michael P, was a tall, nice-looking man with dark hair and brown eyes who had gone to Harvard. He loved teaching and wanted his students to appreciate the law. He stood on the stage with a podium in front of him and would call on us at random to discuss why the rule of law applied to the facts of the cases we were assigned to read the night before. If he was not satisfied with your answer, he would call on another student to tell him what they thought was the correct reasoning. This process was called the Socratic Method, and it was used in many law schools. I often dreaded that I would be called on, much like the rest of the students, but I soon realized that the way to overcome my fear was to be prepared.

During these four weeks, I would go back to my apartment at the end of the day and sit on my bed with my head leaning back against the headboard, thinking about how happy I was to be in this law school. I had tears of happiness running down my cheeks, and I experienced a feeling of peace and comfort in knowing that I had finally found what I was looking for. It was a feeling that seemed to come from a depth within myself that I never known. I felt grateful to be learning these new skills and ideas, and I felt especially thankful for the encouragement and persistence of the male friends that had brought me to this place.

Sadly, the end of the summer came and shattered my illusion of continuing to pursue my dream at John Marshall Law School. I was having difficulty thinking in the logical manner that lawyers need to go through to prove the reasoning behind their conclusions, and after the final exams I received the dreaded news that I was not accepted into the fall program. My friend Cathy was not accepted either. Now, I had to rethink and re-evaluate my life goals.

With the encouragement and recommendation of Cathy and my male friends, I made the decision to apply to law schools in other states. Cathy decided to apply to law schools in San Diego, California, because she had some relatives living there and she liked this city. I decided I liked Los Angeles better and sent off my applications to the schools there, hoping that I could come back into this dream once more.

# Chapter 27

## The Letter

The letter I had been waiting for was sitting in the mail box, prominently placed on top of the rest of the mail. I had heard that the answer I had been yearning to know was supposed to arrive today, one which was going to change my life forever. My heart was racing, my hands were shaking, and my stomach felt tight. Did I want to open the letter now? Perhaps I should wait until after dinner so if the news wasn't good I could just go to bed and cry with disappointment. No, I shouldn't wait. I needed to face what I feared most: rejection.

My fingers struggled to open the envelope, and my eyes were becoming blurry with the fear of what I would find inside. The letter began:

"Dear Ms. Phelan, we are pleased to inform you that you have been selected to join Southwestern Law School in the fall semester, 1980. Congratulations, and we will be sending you information regarding housing in the next week."

I could not believe what I was reading. I did it! I was going to law school! I rushed to the telephone and called the friends who had encouraged and supported this career change to share the wonderful news.

How do I tell my children that I would be moving to California? How would they take this news? How could I move and attend law school without a job? Where was I going to live? Applying to this school had been such a long shot that I didn't even consider what would happen if I was accepted. I had about six months before school started, though, so I had time to figure out how I was going to make this career change become a reality.

I called Patrick and Liz the next day to arrange for us to get together for a weekend in the city. My throat was dry, and the words were hard to get out without saying too much over the phone.

We met at my apartment the following day and went to the Hyatt Hotel for dinner. Once we came back and had a chance to relax, I decided it was time to tell them. I said, "Pat and Liz, I have something I need to share with the both of you. Remember when I told you that I was applying to law school for a career change? Well I was accepted at a school in Los Angeles, California."

Pat said, "No! You didn't!" His face scrunched up as if he were about to cry, but his lip quivered as he held back his emotions.

"So, does this mean you are going to move there?" Liz cried out. "No! I am going to tell them not to accept you!"

They both got up from their chairs and went outside, and their anger was palpable. I felt sick to my stomach. I knew this was going to be an emotional conversation, but after seeing my children's reactions, I began to feel like I was a bad mother. What kind of mother leaves her children to pursue a career that will take her out of state for several years? Sometimes

I asked myself why I was leaving my children to pursue law, and I could not answer this question at the time. However, I knew in my heart and soul that I needed to follow and trust my instincts, and that this was my path regardless of what others thought it should be. Sometimes I think we need to trust in our intuition, even if it makes no sense at the time.

Later, I talked on the phone to Ed and we discussed our options. He was adamant that the kids would not move to California with me, and I agreed. In reality, I did not want Patrick and Liz to be uprooted and taken to a place I knew nothing about. If I was going to pursue this plan, I needed to go alone. However, we agreed that they would come with me for a week when I first moved so they could see where I was living.

When I awoke on the day I would move to California, I felt scared and anxious—just like I have so many other times in my life. My stomach was in knots, and I wanted to go back under the covers to make my anxiety go away. Was I really going to move to California? Oh my God, I hoped I was not making a huge mistake.

Patrick and Elizabeth came with me to the O'Hare Airport, and soon after we arrived at our gate I heard over the loud speaker, "Ms. Phelan, please come to the information desk." My anxiety told me something was wrong. I was not a frequent traveler; my children and I had not traveled by airplane except for two flights to New York to see our family. This was my first time being called up to the desk, and I wasn't sure what to expect. I got up from my seat and looked back at Patrick and Elizabeth, telling them it would be okay while not really believing it myself.

When I got up to the desk, I was given some amazing news: we had been upgraded to first class! I was astounded. I had never been in first class before, and I was so happy to be sharing this experience with Patrick and Elizabeth. Perhaps this was a sign that I had made the right decision after all.

Once we got on the plane, my children were sat in the aisle to my left. On my immediate right was a tall, handsome man with blond hair and beautiful blue eyes. At first, we sat in silence, but after a few hours, Jim—the man sitting next to me—turned to me and said, "Are you visiting family in LA?" We got to talking, and I learned that Jim was an executive with Capital Airlines and was on his way back from visiting family in Chicago. He was living in LA with a female friend and was into competing in marathons all over the world. Patrick and Elizabeth kept glancing over at me several times during this conversation, and I wondered what was going through their minds as they watched their mom talking to this total stranger. Personally, I was amazed that I already met someone who lived in Los Angeles before I had even left the plane.

After we landed, Jim gave me his card and said, "Please, call me anytime." I did not have my new telephone number yet, so the ball was in my court. I dated Jim a short time after we met on the airplane, and he was a very nice guy. However, once I started law school I became invested in my studies and decided that dating was not my focus at this time in my life. Jim understood this very well, and we remained friends.

Patrick, Elizabeth, and I got a taxi from LA to the mid-Wilshire area where my apartment was located, about six blocks from Southwestern Law School and down the street from the Ambassador Hotel where Robert Kennedy was shot. My historic interest was a minor consideration; in truth, I mostly looked for an apartment with a health club nearby so I could continue to have a place to work out my stress. I did not get to see the exact apartment I would be renting when I had first visited Los Angeles a few months prior, but I did get a sense of how far I needed to walk to get to the school. I did not want to rely on a car as I wasn't going to have a job, which meant I needed to live frugally until I got my bearings as a law student. However, I always knew in the back of my mind that I could find a job as a nurse if I needed extra cash.

As we opened the front door of my one-bedroom apartment to find palm trees swaying back and forth in the background, I thought, *I am really here in California.*

I looked at Patrick and Elizabeth and I could see that they were travel weary. Unfortunately, the place wasn't very well set up at the moment—the moving company had left all the boxes from my apartment in Chicago in the middle of the living room! Thankfully the bedroom furniture and the pull-out sofa were set up, so Patrick and Elizabeth had a choice of where to sleep. We placed a few cups and saucers in the kitchen cabinets to be used the next day and headed off to bed.

The next morning, I thought I would get up early and have my usual cup of coffee before the kids awoke. However, upon waking I discovered that the apartment was infested with cockroaches! I screamed, waking up Patrick and Elizabeth in the process. This was not a good beginning for the three of us. I called the apartment supervisor, and of course he acted as if he knew nothing of this situation. He said he would send someone to spray my apartment, and I wanted so much to believe him since there was no one else who would be able to help me.

I did not want this cockroach problem to take away the fun trip I had planned, so I decided to trust that it would be taken care of and headed off on our tour through Disney World, the Hollywood Bowl, and Universal Studios. We spent some time in Santa Monica at the beach and at the Ambassador Hotel. The kids seemed to enjoy their time with me, yet I was aware that they were also sad and anxious about the fact that I wouldn't be coming home with them. I tried to let them talk about their feelings without putting too much pressure on them, which I felt went fairly well—after all, they were thirteen and sixteen, and both of them had already expressed their feelings and thoughts to me before the move.

We had a wonderful week together, but then the time came for Patrick and Elizabeth to leave. It was heartbreaking for me to see the both of them go back to Chicago, and I knew this was twice as difficult for them. I promised to call them often and sent them back home with a heavy heart.

Our family went through a rough adjustment period after my move. Patrick stopped playing football, one of his favorite sports, and I felt so sad and guilty that my decision was affecting my son. Luckily, Ed had several conversations with Patrick's football coach about the life changes he was going through, and he was able to continue playing on the team despite his absences.

Soon after, Ed told me he realized that I was never coming back to him and that he had decided he was going to marry Norma, a woman whom he had been seeing for a year. Patrick and Elizabeth liked Norma and her three children, who were slightly younger, and they had been having a lot of fun together during the past year. On February 14, 1981—Patrick's seventeenth birthday—Ed married Norma in a small family celebration.

Around this time, Ed asked me to claim my portion of our home in Downers Grove. He told me he would pay me the one-half ownership value of our home so he and Norma could move in together, and after I had a real estate friend give her objective evaluation of our home, Ed and I proceeded with this arrangement.

Not long after Ed and Norma married, Elizabeth called me, upset. She said, "Mom, I really want to come and live with you. Norma has removed all the sunflower wallpaper that you put up in our kitchen. It is like she is erasing you from our home."

I felt so sad and helpless because I knew that if I were in Norma's position, I would probably want to do the same thing. However, I also could feel Liz's pain of seeing her stepmother come in and take over the house that she had lived in with me for nine years. I told Liz that I could understand how she felt, but that I also could understand why Norma wanted to make the house feel more like it was hers. I told her, "Liz, I am your mother, and no one can take that away. Norma can change the wallpaper, but I love you, and no one can take this love away from us as mother and daughter. And Liz, if I thought you would be better off with me here in Los Angeles, I would have you with me in a heartbeat. But I am so unsettled right now, and I do not want to have your life be so uncertain. I am hoping to do well here in law school and move back to Chicago to finish my law studies."

Liz listened to me as usual and agreed with me, being the good girl that she was and wanting to please her mom and dad.

This was a difficult time for the both of us. Liz and I had a good relationship with one another, but there was no getting away from the guilt I felt about leaving Liz and Patrick. I did my best to make sure they knew I loved them, and I tried to keep our communication open by letting them know I was there for them whenever they needed me. I hoped that someday, when they were older, they would look back on this time and see it not only as me leaving them, but as me following my heart to pursue my passion, something I have always encouraged them to do.

Years later, Patrick decided to leave a highly-desired position at a top accounting firm in California to pursue his master's degree in business at New York University. When explaining the decision to me, he said, "Mom, the people at work think I should stay at this position to be on the partnership track and not pursue my MBA, but that's not what I want. I remember when you moved to California to attend law school that others did not agree with your decision, but you did it anyway. Like you, I think this is the right choice for me."

I was so proud of him, and I was honored that he emulated my life decision from when he was a teenager. He gained the confidence and inner strength to follow his heart and to pursue his dream, regardless of what others felt was right for him.

Liz also sent me cards over the years expressing how proud she was of me and saying that I was a role model for her. She followed her own heart and worked hard to become the established, professional, licensed social worker she is today.

This is a moment where I can see that I managed to break the cycle of dysfunction that was happening in my family. My relationship with Patrick and Liz was definitely better than the one I had with my mother, and the one my mother had with her own mother, because we did not have the anger and lack of respect for one another. Despite the fact that I chose to do something that would make my children unhappy, I acknowledged the pain they felt and allowed them to express their feelings about this move. I took responsibility for my actions and their outcomes, and I gave them time to realize that this decision didn't diminish how much I loved them. Despite the challenges we faced, the physical separation brought us even closer together as a family.

# Chapter 28

## Law School

I started the night school program at Southwestern Law School in mid-August 1980, attending classes four nights a week from 7:00 PM to 10:00 PM. I loved the challenge that these classes provided. There were about one hundred students in the program, and only twenty percent of the class were women. We also had almost exclusively male professors with the exception of our legal writing class. This was in sharp contrast to my nursing schools, in which women made up about ninety five percent of the class and all of the instructors. This new experience was a welcome change, and I found the energy in a mixed-gender classroom exhilarating.

In the first week of class, we were told by our professors to look to the right, and then to the left, and then they said, "In the next year, fifty percent of you will not be here." I was so sure that I would be among the people that stayed; I was determined to do well so I could go back to Chicago and be with my children. I also felt I had a slight advantage as I had saved enough money to get through a couple of months without working so I could focus on my studies. I didn't want to repeat my experience at the John Marshall Law School in Chicago

The night of our first class, we were all sizing each other up on some subconscious level. I read a book several years ago called *Contact: The First Four Minutes* that described how we unconsciously decide whether or not to talk to another person in a crowd by the way they dress, look, walk, and talk within the first four minutes of noticing them. Personally, I was consciously looking for classmates that I thought I would like to know, but it was all a bit overwhelming. I needed to start somewhere, so I decided to sit in the middle of the class and just wait and see who sat next to me.

We were given a class exercise during this first week that involved choosing ten other classmates and gathering in a small group. We were told that we were going to re-create the Donner Party and experience how we choose who would die due to lack of food and water. I do not recall all the details of this exercise, but I do remember that our study group was formed as a result.

Over the next few days, we began to choose whom we sat with based on whom we had gotten to know. This became important because the people we sat down next to in the classes became our seating partners for the next year, although we didn't know it at the time. Each of the law professors made a seating chart for their classes to refer to when they called out our names, not only for attendance but also for class legal questions using the Socratic Method, a practice that still filled me with dread.

I was fortunate to sit next to Beth, who worked as an executive in Hollywood. Beth and I immediately became best friends. It is interesting to note that we were both about the same height and weight—we looked like we could be sisters. We both wore white silk shirts and black pants. We had dark brown hair and an attitude of confidence. She loved showing me around Los Angeles, and she owned her own home in the Hollywood Hills. She was about ten years younger than me and had never married. Beth was Jewish, and she invited me to all the Jewish holiday events that fall.

After a week of classes, we were encouraged to meet as a group with other classmates to get together and study. Beth and I joined up with Bob, who was interested in railroad law; Tim, who became my male best friend and worked as a manager of a law firm; Jane, who was a court reporter; Susan, a set designer; and Michael, a free agent. They were all single—that is, until Beth and Michael became a couple—and had no children. The average age in this group was thirty years old, and I was thirty-eight. The group decided to meet once a week at my apartment since I did not have a car to travel to their homes, which were spread out all over the Los Angeles area. We would go over our class lessons. I was not used to studying in a group and found it to be a frustrating use of my time; I had trouble focusing on the issues and was distracted by the opinions of other members of the group. The positive side of this activity, though, was the social relationships we formed with one another.

While the study group was going well overall, I was struggling emotionally because I missed my children. I found it hard to focus, and I was not as intellectually prepared for law school as I had hoped I would be. Money was also becoming an issue. I loved not working at first, but I did not enjoy having no income. I was used to a higher-end lifestyle, and the apartment complex I was living in was in a sketchy area.

In November 1980 I decided to apply for a part-time position as a law clerk at a firm just blocks away from my apartment, and I was hired immediately. It was a defense firm primarily involved in accident cases that had a good reputation in the area, and they were very gracious in acknowledging my nursing background and treating me with warmth and respect. I felt like I was a valued member of the law firm. Unfortunately, I realized after the Christmas holidays that I had taken on more than I could handle. I did not do well on my first final exams, and I felt overwhelmed. I had to resign from the firm so I could focus on school. To this day, I still appreciate the manner in which the law firm treated me, even though I was only there a short time.

At the end of my first semester I received a total point average of 74.5, just half a point short of passing, so I was placed on probation for my second semester. This was very difficult for me because I wanted to transfer back to a law school in Illinois so I could be near my children, and my grades needed to be higher for that to be an option. I knew I would have to step things up for my second round of final exams.

In April of 1981, I used the money I had received from Ed buying me out of our home to purchase a two-bedroom condominium on Trevino Drive in Valencia, California. I was happy to finally own a condo and have a sense of home. However, I needed to work in order to pay the mortgage for the condo and for the car I would need to travel both to work and law school, which took about two hours a day. I tried to rationalize my decision by buying tapes on the subjects I was studying to use my driving time more efficiently.

Between my move to Valencia and my sadness around missing my children, the second semester did not start off well. When I sat down to study, I would get distracted by noises outside or my thoughts would wander to my children and how they were doing. Studying also brought back feelings of guilt for not attending my grandfather's funeral when I was sixteen years old because I had to stay home and study for my final exams. Now, I had the added guilt of leaving my two children behind to study law. I wondered, what were they doing? How were they feeling? When would I get the time to see them? I called them every week, but I had not seen them since last August—I could not afford the plane fare, or the time. Tears fell from my eyes onto the page, making concentration impossible.

In May 1981, I applied for the position of nurse coordinator at the Neuropsychiatric Institute at UCLA, and I was accepted to the position and started working full time that same July. My weekdays were now full between work and law classes, and so my weekends became my time to study. And still, when I sat down on my sofa and tried to focus, my thoughts would wander to Patrick and Elizabeth. Law school was not progressing as I had thought it would.

## Chapter 29

### Living with Failure

In July 1981, a letter arrived stating that I was disqualified from studying at the Southwestern University School of Law due to my academic performance. I felt sick about the loss of this dream and disappointed with myself for being unable to pass my law exams. How did this happen to me? What was I going to tell my kids, family, and friends? No, I thought, I cannot give up now. I decided to take a deep breath, go for a run, and give this disappointment some thought.

The letter said I had the option to appeal this decision and ask to be reinstated for the next academic year, and that is the route I decided to go. I had received the second-highest grade in my contracts class, so I asked the professor if he could write a letter stating I had the ability to do well in my studies. I also wrote my own letter about my personal life challenges that I felt contributed to my poor performance, such as my move from Chicago and leaving my two children behind. Thankfully, my petition was granted.

As I was waiting to see if my appeal would be accepted, I

shared this academic failure with my friend Cathy, who was in law school in San Diego, and my friend Diane, who was a doctoral student in nursing in Chicago. They were wonderful friends who gave me the support I needed to get through this difficult time by accepting me for who I was. They both said to me, "I love you for who you are as my friend, not for how successful you feel you need to be." I did mention what was happening to my mother and father, and while they listened to me and supported me as much as they could, neither of them could relate to how I felt since they had never experienced this kind of drive to pursue a dream.

While my school life was in a downswing, my personal life saw a noticeable improvement. In early June 1981 I received a phone call from Jim—the young man I met on the plane when I first moved to Los Angeles—asking if I would be interested working for Capitol Airlines on an as-needed basis as a representative in small claims court. As an employee of the airlines, I would able to fly standby to Chicago for free. I of course said yes, grateful to be offered this incredible opportunity. This was an unbelievable gift—I had not been able to see my children since they flew to California with me the previous August.

I called Patrick and Liz right away, and when Liz answered I said, "What are you both doing this weekend?"

She responded, "We have not thought about it yet, why?"

"Well, how would you like Mom to come to Chicago for a few days to see the both of you?"

Liz shrieked with delight and shouted to Patrick to come to the phone. Patrick was also happy, but being a typical seventeen-year-old he simply said, "That's cool, Mom." We made plans for me to visit them the following weekend.

My heart swelled with love when I saw my children at the

O'Hare Airport; it was hard for me to believe we had been apart for almost a year. They had changed and grown so much taller, and they were both so much more mature than I remembered. I cried as I ran to hug them.

We spent the next four days together at a hotel in downtown Chicago and we enjoyed catching up. I told them about my academic disappointment and explained that I would not be able to transfer back to Chicago due to my grades. However, I also told them the good news that we could now fly to see one another much more easily, and that I planned on coming back to watch Patrick's football games.

Leaving them to go back to Los Angeles was emotional for me, and for them. I wanted to set a date to come back before I left, but I could not plan that far ahead. I had two summer classes that ran until the end of July, and I would be starting my new nursing position at the UCLA neuropsychiatric hospital almost immediately after. However, it was still a relief to know that we could now easily see one another whenever we wanted.

My drive to UCLA to begin my first day of work once again felt like I was going home; the place I would be working was very similar to Rush University in Chicago. As I walked along the campus of the university on this warm summer day, I wondered what experiences would await me. I thought about how much I had learned and changed since my first job in psychiatry as a night charge nurse in 1971. Now I was a struggling law student in beautiful Los Angeles and the mother of two teenage children, preparing to enter another unknown experience.

As I opened the locked door to my new professional home, I took a deep breath and reminded myself about what I would be doing. I was hired as an administrative nurse on a twenty-one-bed adult acute psychiatric inpatient unit. I had total responsibility for all nursing care delivered by a staff, which consisting of eighteen registered nurses, four and a half psychiatric technicians, and one mental health practitioner. I was also responsible for the clinical supervision of two UCLA graduate students from community mental health and worked closely with their instructor during their student placement on the unit. Later, after a glowing recommendation from my nursing supervisor, I was also appointed as a faculty member of the UCLA School of Nursing.

I believe my continued success in nursing and the support I received from my supervisors helped me withstand the failure I was experiencing in law school. However, I also believe that the ease with which I had achieved my success in nursing made it hard for me to accept my failure. I believe that where there is a will, there is a way, but so far I hadn't found my way.

In retrospect, I can see a subtle pattern in my nursing positions that seems to prevail throughout my nursing career. My nursing supervisors were always very positive and supportive of me, but some of the nursing staff working under me would have issues with me as a leader. An example of this came from my new position at the neuropsychiatric hospital. The prior nursing coordinator had had a very close social relationship with the staff, going out for drinks and maintaining friendships with them outside of the work environment. In contrast, my personal belief was that I should not be socializing with the staff outside of work because it could blur the emotional issues that can occur in this type of setting. Staying impartial would help me objectively evaluate my staff, and I had more important issues to deal with than getting caught up in the personal issues of the staff. In addition to missing my children and trying to find time to study for my law classes, I was having to be an objective mediator for my nursing staff so they could provide excellent patient care.

I discovered shortly after I started working on the unit that the cute, spunky, vivacious registered nurse whom I had immediately taken a liking to felt that she should be in my position, despite being ten years my junior and not having a master's degree. She had worked on the unit for several years and was not only romantically involved with the mental health worker but was also a very close friend of the unit director. She tried to undermine me from the beginning by telling the other staff members that my ideas would not work. At first, I was not aware of what she was doing, but I recognized this subtle dynamic after several months of meeting with my management team every month on a supervisory basis.

I decided to deal with the situation by including her in my decision-making process. I would ask her what she thought of my ideas during the leadership meetings that I held twice a month. This meant that she could either speak up and give me her ideas or be quiet, putting an end to her ability to undermine me because she was forced to say what she thought in front of the entire staff.

I believed in a cooperative team approach, not an autocratic one like these nurses had previously experienced. I empowered the nursing staff to have a say in what kind of patients should be admitted to the unit and how their monthly work schedule should be determined. The result was that they had more control over their work environment, which led to a greater satisfaction in their everyday work and greater patient satisfaction.

On my way to work at UCLA in the spring of 1982, I had the impulse to fly home to Massapequa Park to visit my parents, and to see my grandfather's gravesite. I was having difficulty with my law school exams due to my unresolved grief reaction to my grandfather's death, and even though the trip would be overwhelming time-wise I knew it was something I needed to do. In early April I flew back home and went with my father to my paternal grandfather's grave. It was a perfect spring day—there was no humidity, the sun was shining brightly, and there was no wind. My mother did not come with us, which was unusual because my mother never seemed to allow us to be alone together. Perhaps she still felt that drive to keep a distance between us.

We drove into the large cemetery filled with tall trees and stopped at the office to pick up a map. My father and I were both quiet, as was our nature, while we looked for the signpost that would show us where my beloved grandparents were buried. It took us a while to find the right plot.

Once we found it, my father just stood there with me in silence. The sun was shining brightly, and then suddenly a gush of wind began swirling around the tombstone. "What was that?" I cried out. My father just held me, and I began sobbing. There was no doubt in my mind that this was some kind of spiritual message. I later learned through psychotherapy while reflecting on this time, that it was likely a letting go of my grandfather's spirit. It was truly unbelievable and beautiful at the same time.

My father and I drove back to the house together, still in silence. I always thought I had all of these unanswered questions for my father, but after this day together, I realized I had nothing I wanted to ask him. I was content to just BE with my father; nothing else mattered.

Two days later, my parents drove me to the airport. My father insisted that we drive by my grandparents' old house in Uniondale along the way. I did not want to do this; a part of me wanted to remember the house as I did as a child, not at is was now. I could hardly recognize the neighborhood of the home

I remembered with such love and fondness; so many of the houses had changed. My grandparents' house had stayed the same, at least externally. It was the same off-white color, with the closed-in porch in the front that I remembered sleeping in when I was seven. However, I knew this house was not the same on the inside because my grandparents were no longer there. In retrospect, I believe that my father wanted to see the house with me after all these years because he had a sense of nostalgia after we visited the grave site of his father. He wanted to share this memory with me, knowing how close to him I had been.

Once we arrived at the airport, I kissed my mother and father goodbye. As I left the car and walked to the gate, I had a thought that I would never see my father again. There were no signs to indicate there was anything wrong with him, so I dismissed the thought and headed back to California. Having cleared what was holding me back, I was ready to tackle law school once more.

# Chapter 30

## I Am Not the Girl I Used to Be

My brother Sonny and I both have a vivid memory from the morning of June 25, 1982. We were working at our jobs, he in New York and I in California, and we had a vague sense of not feeling well—a feeling that something was wrong. We each thought that maybe it was the beginning of the flu, or that we ate something that did not agree with us. Unbeknownst to one another, we both left work early due to this feeling.

As I entered my condo, I heard the phone ringing. It was Sonny, sobbing, and he told me that our father had died at sixty-four years of age. He had been on his way to work when he had a heart attack while driving. His car was found on the side of the road. The sheriff tried to revive him with CPR, but he was unsuccessful. The autopsy report showed he'd had a prior heart attack that no one knew about and that three of his arteries were ninety-eight percent occluded. This was a shock to our entire family. My father was the second youngest of six brothers, and all of them were healthy.

After the phone call, I was in a state of disbelief. How

could this happen? Did my mother know there was something wrong with him? Didn't she see any signs that he was in pain? I could not move off of my sofa; I could only stare straight out my floor-to-ceiling glass doors and watch my huge willow tree gently sway with the breeze. It didn't seem real that he was gone.

A few hours later, I called my mother to see how she was doing. Sonny had told me she was quite upset and was making funeral arrangements with my twenty-two-year-old brother Guy and some of her close friends. The phone call was painful—she was sobbing and at times hysterical. I promised to come home as soon as I could get a flight out of Los Angeles, and she replied in between sobs, "Thank God you came back here to see your father before he died." All I could do was cry.

The next phone call I had to make was to Patrick and Elizabeth to inform them about their grandfather's death. I felt so tired and dreaded giving them this sad news over the phone since Patrick, eighteen, and Elizabeth, fifteen, were close to him when they were children. I decided to first call Ed so he could be prepared to support the kids and so we could decide what day was best to bring them to the airport. We then got the both of them on the phone at the same time so they could hear the news together. They were sad and said they wanted to go to New York to attend the funeral, so I made travel arrangements for their flights and had relatives pick them up at JFK.

As I look back on the weekend of my father's funeral, I can see how I just went through the motions for everything I did. I was there, but I was also not there. I recall being so tired and that all I wanted to do was sleep. I could not talk with anyone other than my children. My mother had friends and family around which was a relief, because I could not be there for her. It was a sad and painful time for all of us, and I felt incapable of caring for anyone else.

There had been so much loss in our family in the past four years. My children personally experienced the loss of their family life and their childhood as they once knew it with Ed and my divorce. This loss was further exacerbated when I moved to California two years later. In retrospect, I can see that I was unconsciously carrying on this legacy of loss through my choices in life as a mother.

Both my maternal and paternal grandparents and family had suffered the loss of a child. While I did not suffer the loss of a child, Patrick and Liz experienced another kind of loss. In trying to protect them from life's pain and sorrow, I instead added to their pain and sorrow through my decision to divorce their dad and move away from them to attend law school. I was far from a perfect mother, and it seems like the more I wanted to spare them the kind of pain I felt as a child, the more I created a different kind of pain for them through my decisions as their mother. I wanted with all my heart to protect them from a world that is fragile.

The day of my father's funeral reminded me that everything cherished can vanish in an instant. I was so happy to have Patrick and Elizabeth with me and for them to be at their grandfather's funeral as I did not want them to miss this important event. Patrick, Liz, and I sat together at the funeral home and walked up to the casket to say our goodbyes.

I cried all the way through my flight home and continued to feel numb. I thought about all the times I wanted to make my father proud of me by playing sports because he had been a star football player in high school. I realized I was seeking his attention, my actions shouting "Daddy, Daddy, look at me!" Now, he was gone, and I was no longer the girl I used to be. Over the following weeks, I continued to go through my everyday activities in a flat and lifeless manner. I stopped going to the gym, and I felt no enjoyment from anything that I once loved to do. I needed time to figure out what I was going to do with my life.

After several months of adjusting to my losses, I recalled a physician acquaintance at Rush University who was going to law school by correspondence. He had been very encouraging of my pursuing law school when I was in Chicago and had given me several of his law text books to use when I started the program. I decided to look into the 1983 fall program at Southland University. If I was accepted, I would be able to take courses that worked around my schedule and still obtain my Juris Doctor degree. Also, the Committee of Bar Examiners accepted my prior two and a half years of law studies from Southwestern University, which meant I would only need to complete an additional one and a half years through the correspondence program to meet the academic eligibility for the California bar exam. I was accepted, and I once again had a direction and goal to obtain my law degree. I may not be the girl I used to be, but I was a stronger and wiser woman striving toward my goal.

The best day I remember having in the year after my father died came when I received a phone call from Elizabeth. "Mom, guess what? We are moving to California this summer!"

"Are you serious?" I shouted, beside myself with joy at this fantastic news.

"I am! Dad has been transferred to Walnut Creek, so we will be moving there in the summer as soon as school is out."

After the phone call, I went for a walk around the golf course which surrounded my condo complex, looked up at the beautiful blue sky, and thanked God for this beautiful gift. I would finally be close to my children again.

# Chapter 31

## Finding My Stride

At the end of summer of 1983, just a few months after my children moved to California, Patrick called me and said, "Mom, I don't want to stay in California. I hate all the sunshine, and I don't want to go back to university. I've decided to go back to New Jersey to live with Aunt Pat and Uncle Jerry for a while. Uncle Jerry said I could work in his sheet metal business."

I was so surprised to hear this from Patrick because he was always a good student and had been very clear on his career goals. He had completed his first year at Marquette University in Wisconsin at the end of May, just a few weeks before Ed moved the family to Walnut Creek. However, Pat was upset about the move and at his dad for selling his childhood home. They had moved into a nice home and neighborhood, but at nineteen Pat was having a hard time adjusting. I strongly supported his decision, as did Ed, knowing that he was doing what was best for him.

In looking back at this time, I can understand that for Patrick, the sale of his childhood home had hit him like an earthquake. He had gone through the divorce of his parents at age eleven, my move to downtown Chicago four years later, my move to California two years after that, his dad remarrying on his seventeenth birthday, and the recent loss of his grandfather. Now the home that had been the very foundation he knew and depended on during some of the most formative years of his life was gone, and he was shaken by this change. I believe these losses had a more profound effect on him than any of us realized. I felt I was partly to blame for his anguish since it was my life choices that resulted in most of the losses he was experiencing, and while Pat did not blame me, I hoped that one day he would forgive me and understand how much I loved him.

Elizabeth, age sixteen, was also struggling a bit as well. She was happy to be living in the same state as I was, but she missed her friends. Thankfully, she met a friend at school named Scott who also was new to the area—he was from Australia and had moved to be with his dad. They both connected immediately and are friends to this day.

After Ed moved to Walnut Creek, I loved to drive up from Los Angeles whenever possible to spend some time with my children. One day, after Patrick moved to New Jersey, I called Elizabeth to tell her that I was thinking of visiting her and asked if she would be willing to meet me for lunch. She was elated and said she could not wait to see me.

I drove from Los Angeles to Walnut Creek in five hours, listening to jazz music while letting my mind wander. When I arrived at the family's new home, Liz answered the door immediately. She wanted me to see her new room, and I could see that she loved showing me around the house. We enjoyed talking about her new school and her friend Scott. She had met a few girlfriends who lived nearby, but she still missed her friends from Illinois.

The afternoon went by very quickly, and unfortunately, I had to drive back to Los Angeles that day because I had to work the following day. However, it was worth the trip to spend time with Elizabeth. We continued to have a close relationship, and it was such a delight to be with one another. Despite the challenges in her life, I never sensed in Liz the angst I had with my own mother. As I left, we agreed to see one another on a more frequent basis.

When the fall season was coming to an end, Patrick was feeling better after spending some time in New Jersey and decided to come back to California for a short time during the Christmas holidays. Elizabeth was so happy to spend time with him. I was able to take another day trip to be with Patrick and Elizabeth for the Christmas holiday, and it was wonderful to have that time together.

During the spring of 1984, I was still busy with my two law school classes, my full-time position as a nursing coordinator, and my position on the faculty of the UCLA School of Nursing. Then, one afternoon, my nursing supervisor called me into the assistant director's office. She said, "I recently met the current Dean of Nursing for the Antelope Valley College, and she is looking for someone to replace her since she was recently promoted to vice president. I think you would be perfect for this position, and it would get you out of the hospital setting in preparation for your future law career." I was not expecting this offer at all. Since it was a Friday afternoon, she suggested I think about it over the weekend. I told her I would give it some thought, although I did not want to make any further changes in my career at this time; I already had a full plate.

As I tried to come to a decision, I read the job description and could not believe that she thought I was qualified for this position. Jane was very persuasive, though, and eventually I decided I would go for the interview. My attitude was to simply hear what they had to say and answer any questions that were asked of me without putting too much pressure on myself.

Antelope Valley College was located seventy-five miles from my condo in Valencia, but the good news was that there was no traffic going this way in that direction on the highway. I arrived at the college for my interview with the president, and as I walked down the halls I felt as if I was in school again. When I found the room I was looking for, I noticed there were five people sitting around a table; I had expected to meet with only the president. I took a deep breath and walked into the room with confidence, and everyone stood up as I approached the table. After the president introduced himself, he said, "I decided to have some of the nursing faculty here today so you would not have to drive here for another interview. I hope this is okay with you." I told him I was fine with his decision, and that I appreciated him saving me another drive. He then introduced the members of the nursing team and said I could ask any of them any questions I might have regarding the program.

We all got seated around the table, and the first question they asked was, "Why do I want this position?"

I almost laughed at this question. I instantly relaxed and sat forward with my arms outstretched on the table in front of me. "I am so happy you asked me this question," I said, "because in all honesty I did not seek this position. I am here at the request of my supervisor, Jane. I love my position at UCLA and I am simply here to find out about you and your program and hear what you are looking for." They smiled and proceeded to discuss the specifics of what the position entailed and what they were looking for in a dean of allied health. They asked if I was offered the position, could I guarantee that I would stay on for three years? I said that I could.

The interview ended up being fun for me, and I enjoyed the process more than I anticipated. I liked the president and the nursing staff; they seemed like they would be good people to work with.

I was offered the position two days later, and it took me a while to digest this news. The more I thought about it, though, the more excited and enthusiastic I felt. This position would give me the opportunity to give back to nursing, since my nursing career was what had gotten me to where I was today. The new school year would start in four months, so I would have time to readjust my study plans and have my nursing supervisor find a replacement for me. I called back and accepted the offer.

One of my first responsibilities as the dean was to interview each student that qualified to be accepted into the program. It did not seem so long ago that I was a young mother desperately trying to achieve my goal of becoming a nurse, and now I was now on the other side helping young women fulfill their dreams. I had come full circle.

My first week as a dean was a very busy yet enjoyable time for me. It was fun to be on a college campus again, and I loved my new office—it was located toward the back of the building, which provided some privacy. Of the five deans on campus, I was the only female. The prior dean, who was now the vice president of academic affairs, was also a nurse and had been an excellent role model to the staff, so I had some big shoes to fill.

With this role came the expectation that I would be involved in the community as a speaker and representative of the college. I was also required to be a member of many nursing organizations and committees that dealt with health care throughout the state. I went on local TV to discuss the available nursing programs and presented seminars such as "Health Care: Dealing with Difficult Emotional/Legal Dilemmas" and

"Critical Issues in Health Care." I also participated in a press conference to discuss the college's involvement in and support for the Emergency Technology Program in Bishop.

Soon after I started in this position, I was asked to be an expert witness for a law firm in Beverly Hills; I was referred to the lawyer by a friend from law school who had worked with this firm. It seemed as if my professional world was expanding beyond my wildest dreams. Within a year of beginning my work as a dean, I became a tenured employee and was listed in "Who's Who of American Nursing."

My position with Capital Airlines had been ongoing from the summer of 1981 through to October 1984. Because I got busy with my other work demands, it took me a couple of months to notice that I had not heard from the company in a while. I decided to call and check if there were any recent cases, and to my surprise and astonishment they were no longer in business! I tried to call Jim, but his phone was also disconnected. I never heard or knew what happened to Jim, but I did later learn that Capitol Airlines went bankrupt.

I was amazed that the position lasted for the last three years when I most needed it, and then once I no longer had to fly to see my children the job just seemed to vanish into thin air. The timing was absolutely incredible.

Then, in the early summer of 1984, I received a call from Patrick that I never could have expected. He had decided to come back to California to take some classes, and he asked if he could stay with me. I prepared the second bedroom for him and waited not-so-patiently to have him live with me again; the last time we lived together was six years ago, back in Downers Grove.

One week later, I was pacing the floor in anticipation of his arrival. He had decided to buy himself a motorcycle and was traveling from Walnut Creek to Valencia on the I-5 highway. I had driven on this highway many times, and I was very concerned for him because of the big four-wheel trucks and cars that speed down that long stretch of road. When I heard the sound of a motorcycle coming up the street I ran outside to greet him, elated that he made it safe and sound. We hugged one another, and then I ushered him inside. I knew he would be tired, so we planned on getting him settled and having a quiet dinner and evening. It was wonderful to wake up the next day and know he was here for a few months. We spent the weekend getting Patrick acclimated to Valencia and Brentwood, where UCLA is located.

The 1984 Summer Olympics were being held at the UCLA campus, and Patrick applied for a part-time position as a security guard. He started the position soon after being accepted and enjoyed meeting other college-aged students and interesting people. He completed his classes at a nearby college, and he stayed living with me until January 1985, when he decided to would move back to Walnut Creek to get his major in business administration from the San Francisco State University. My life was enhanced during the time Pat spent with me, and living together again provided us with a deeper mother-son bonding.

On one of our several dinners out at a restaurant, Patrick said, "Remember when Liz and I went to Hawaii with Dad for a conference in 1974?" I told him I remembered that it was a short time after we were separated. He continued, "It was a long flight from Chicago, so we had a long layover in San Francisco. I always remember when I saw San Francisco, I knew I would be living here someday." I listened and smiled because I knew this feeling very well.

After he graduated with his MBA, Patrick was recruited

by several of the Big Five accounting firms. They took him to dinner, brought him on boat rides, and offered many other perks. After graduation, he chose to work with Ernst and Young in Newport Beach, California, and completed his CPA exams within the next two years. He found his own place and moved just forty minutes away from me. I couldn't be prouder of the man he has become.

# Chapter 32

## Meeting Gary Gwilliam

I decided to leave my position as dean in the summer of 1987 after fulfilling my three-year commitment. I had graduated from Southland Law School in 1985, but since I had been so busy I had not had the time to study to take the bar exam. I now planned on taking the 1988 exam, so I wanted to look for a position that would give me more experience in law. I was fortunate to find a job as a law clerk at a firm that primarily defended psychologists and psychiatrists against plaintiffs who were alleging that they were sexually abused by their doctors. I was fortunate to find this unique position that was an extension of my nursing career in mental health, and I was both excited and challenged by this career change. It was a small boutique law firm located in Newport Beach, California, and the four lawyers in the firm were very supportive of me in my new role.

Unfortunately, I did not pass the bar, and after a year of working at the firm I had to leave because they needed a lawyer to take over in order to bring the many cases to trial. For the next two years, I returned to working as a nursing supervisor in psychiatry, accepting positions at two different hospitals.

By November 1990, I was busy working two jobs and was anxiously awaiting the results of the most recent bar exam, which were to come out the Friday after Thanksgiving. One of the jobs I had at the time was working every Saturday and Sunday from 7:00 AM to 7:00 PM at a psychiatric hospital in Long Beach, California. The beauty of this position was that I received full-time pay with health benefits. There were many staff members who were envious of this position, and they openly told me how they wished they were in my place.

The day would start with a report from the night supervisor, which contained information on how many patients we had in the hospital, how many staff members were on each unit, and any potential patient problems that were likely to occur that day. The hospital had about one hundred patients and was located in an area that had gang-related activities. We also had a number of patients with dissociative disorder that were victims of a satanic cult. My role as supervisor was to make rounds through the various units, talk with the head nurse and some of the patients to see how they were doing, and get a sense of how everything was going. I always had my eyes and ears open, relying on my intuitive sense of my surroundings.

The satanic cult, which was active in the Los Angeles area in the 1980s, was a concern for me. I was not very knowledgeable about this group and was unsure what to expect from them. Several patients claimed to be victims of the cult. Many of these patients had a dissociative disorder, meaning they had multiple personalities as a result of severe life trauma. They would dissociate their life from the real world due to their pain. These patients claimed they had escaped the cult and were in the hospital to get treatment, but they often created chaos in their unit by splitting the staff members into "good guys" and "bad guys."

One day, a staff member stopped by my office and asked to talk with me. He was working with a patient who claimed she was a victim of the cult. He told me that he found a dead cat on his back porch—a warning to him that he was being watched. Thankfully, nothing further came from this unsettling event. This was a frightening time to be around this negative energy, but I felt safe because we had a security guard on the hospital premises at all times, as well as several physically strong, male nurses whom we could call on for assistance.

At this same time, I was working part time as a clinical psychiatric assessment specialist at the Las Encinas Hospital in Pasadena, California. The hospital was known as a private drug and alcohol program for the wealthy and famous, and several popular actors and actresses had been patients there. It was located on several acres of land and was surrounded by beautiful gardens, tall oak trees, Japanese maples, and flowering bushes. It looked more like a resort than a hospital.

The facility was close to where I was living in Glendale, where I had moved to save money on my rent. My responsibilities included doing an initial psychological assessment to determine a prospective patient's eligibility for the program and also identifying family members who needed the intervention. I was the first person that new patients met when they came into the hospital, and after obtaining all of their information I would call the nursing staff to come and bring them to the unit for treatment.

One day, I received an emergency call from a family member who was bringing in her husband. I alerted the nursing staff that the patient was on his way to be admitted involuntarily, and that I would need help getting him out of the car and into the unit.

I could see the car coming down the long tree-lined road to the hospital entrance, and I was unsure how this would go because of his involuntary status. Thankfully, he slowly got out of the car, accompanied by two male relatives. He was forty-five years of age, six feet tall, slim, and handsome. His dark brown eyes looked dazed, and he was confused about where he was. He looked at the people who had brought him there and asked, "What is going on? Where am I?" I stood back and let the two male staff members walk slowly toward him and tell him he was there for alcohol treatment. He did not put up a struggle and allowed the staff members to lead him to the unit for admission. His wife and family members were relieved to have him safe in treatment for at least twenty-eight days, and I was happy the admission went smoothly and hoped he would be successful in the program.

This position was stressful because I never knew from hour to hour if the admittance process would be smooth as the example above or if we would need security to take an uncooperative patient to the unit. This work was tiring, and I only intended to keep it for a short time to help me get by financially as I could not live on the salary of my weekend position. I needed to pass the bar exam so I could find a job I loved that would give me more stability in my life.

I was single at this time, and I actually quite enjoyed it as I did not have to account to anyone in my personal life and could have privacy whenever I wanted it. I was open to entering a relationship, but only if the person truly enhanced my life, which to me meant a successful person who was aware of himself and who loved his job and his life. I wanted someone to complement me in my interests and also support me in my ongoing goals and growth. I had worked hard on myself and did not want to deal with other people's issues unless they were willing to examine their own lives.

On November 1, 1990, I got a notice from the director of nursing at the Long Beach Hospital that they were going through a reorganization and my position was going to be eliminated, starting that day! At first I was in shock, but soon I felt tremendous relief, as if a weight had been lifted from deep within me. Later, I realized that even though I was stressed by the work, I could never have left this position on my own. It had too many benefits, and there were too many people who were telling me how lucky I was to have it. But, now that it no longer existed, I was truly free on my weekends, and I had many plans for what I wanted to do next.

The first thing I wanted to do was to sign up for the California Trial Lawyers Association Convention, which was going to be held two weeks later in La Jolla, California. I had been a student member of the Los Angeles Trial Lawyers Association for a couple of years now and went to their monthly meetings, which I found to be great motivation for me to pass the bar exam and helped me to become familiar with the world of lawyers. The educational programs were informative, and the social networking would be beneficial in my future law career.

I had also become a member of the LA Trial Lawyers Ethics Committee, which was relevant to me because of my background in working with people who were terminally ill. The committee at the time was working on the issue of a patient's right to die. I met Richard Scott, MD, JD, who was a pioneer of physician-assisted suicide for patients who wanted to die due to the quality of his or her life being significantly compromised by physical problems. The legal and ethical issues surrounding this issue were challenging and interesting, and being on the committee satisfied my goal of combining law and nursing.

Having lost my job, I was now free to attend the three-day

convention. I contacted my friend from when I first started law school, Cathy McCrae. She was a teacher now and lived in La Jolla, California, and we would get together every few months. It had been a while since I had last seen her due to our busy schedules, so I was looking forward to getting together with her.

I drove down to La Jolla to attend the convention, but when I called Cathy to make dinner arrangements she told me that she was not feeling well and would not be able to meet with me. I could not believe it! She had always been available for all the years I have known her, and I was so looking forward to our time to catch up with each other. Now what do I do?

I considered attending the cocktail party that was being hosted as part of the convention, but I did not want to go by myself. Even though I had attended events like this alone many times over the past sixteen years while I was single, I just felt a tremendous resistance within myself. I was not in the mood for the small talk that accompanies these events. However, the alternative of spending the night in my hotel room was also not very appealing, so I went against my inner resistance and forced myself to attend.

That night, I entered the large, dimly-lit ballroom with several round tables spread around the room. There were candles on the tables, two separate bar areas on opposite sides of the room with long lines, and a large table in the center with hors d'oeuvres. People were milling around and talking, and I was on the edge of the room trying to decide where to go and who I might recognize that I could talk with.

I decided to get a glass of wine to settle my anxiety, feeling like a stranger in a strange land. As I was standing in line, I saw Steve Pingle, a lawyer I had known and dated a few times. I had not seen him in a while, but we had a very nice and uncomplicated friendship. He came up to say hello, and after our customary greetings he introduced me to a few other friends he was with and invited me to join them at their table. Before long, Bill Newkirk, another lawyer who worked on a lot of medical malpractice cases in Los Angeles, joined us, and we all then proceeded to go to dinner together. We discussed challenges that each person faced in their career and shared stories of vacations and places we wanted to see in the world. This evening was so much more interesting than I previously thought it would be, and I was glad that I had decided to come out.

After dinner, Steve asked me, "How would you like to attend a candlelight meeting with me? This meeting is for lawyers who have had substance abuse or drug related issues. They get together and share how their lives are going. Since you have your psychiatric nursing background, you might find this group interesting." I agreed to go as I thought it would be better than going back to my room, and because I was interested in what these people would say to one another.

The candlelight meeting was located in the same hotel, and we entered a dark room featuring a large round table with a candle burning in the center. Steve ran the group, and there were five guys. I was the only female, and the only one not known to the others. Surprisingly, however, I was not uncomfortable as I sat and listened to the group talk, perhaps thanks to all of my years in psychiatric nursing.

There was one lawyer, Gary Gwilliam, who shared that he had been sober for two years at the time of the meeting. He was fifty-three years old, his life was good, and his career was a success. However, he had just left a nineteen-year marriage six weeks ago, which had been very hard for him to do. He had two teenage girls, and his wife was a wonderful person but they had both become different people. He had been married once before for ten years and had a daughter from that marriage, and he had gone through a nasty divorce that he did not want to repeat. He and his second wife were both in agreement that the marriage was over, and they both sought a therapist to figure out to how to best tell their daughters. He went on to say that the separation was difficult, but now that he was living alone for the first time in his life, he was enjoying using this time to get to know himself. He said he still loved his wife and that they had tried to make it work, but he had changed since he became sober and the two of them were growing in separate ways. His story resonated with my own personal reasons for getting divorced back in 1974. There was no other person involved, and there was no physical abuse nor any alcohol or drugs. I had just outgrown my marriage.

As I listened to him, I was impressed by the integrity that he showed by leaving his marriage. In the sixteen years I had been single I had come to know and date some very successful men, mostly doctors and lawyers since they were part of my professional world. I was well aware how many married men thought nothing of having an affair and often did not leave their wives unless there was another woman waiting on the side. Gary Gwilliam did not know me and there was no reason for him not to be honest with his friends, so I believed he was telling the full story. I spoke up and said, "I am very impressed with the way you and your wife handled your divorce and how you carefully prepared your children for this important change in their lives. I wish you well, but know that it will take time for all of you to make this huge adjustment in your lives."

The meeting ended, and as we all left the room a few others joined the small group. One of them was Gary's law partner, Jim Chiosso. Gary introduced me, since we had met one another in the group, and then we all went our separate ways since it was getting to be quite late. I returned to my room, and as I thought over the events of the evening I was bemused with how the evening had gone, despite my earlier apprehension.

I left my hotel early Sunday morning to return home, and as I drove I reflected on the weekend and my time at the convention. Surprisingly, my thoughts brought me to the candle light meeting and Gary Gwilliam. I thought about how I had seen him at a luncheon the day of our meeting, where he had presented an award to the past president, Buddy Herzog. As Gary was about to leave the stage, Buddy had moved to the microphone and said, "Gary, do not leave yet, we have an award for you." Gary had looked surprised as he came back to the center of the stage and Buddy handed him an award on behalf of the California Trial Lawyers Association for his prior year as president. Everyone at the luncheon had stood up and applauded him for his very difficult year. I did not know him, but as a member of this group I could sense the warmth and respect the people in the room had for him and his leadership. He seemed like a very nice man, but he also was a recently separated recovering alcoholic who lived in Oakland, which was five hundred miles away from me.

I tried to push my thoughts about him out of my mind, but as I drove further, a voice inside me was saying, *Call him.* I thought I would come to my senses once I got back home and had work to distract me, but these thoughts persisted. I had plans to see my therapist the next day to work on the block I was experiencing around the bar exam, so I decided that I would discuss this dilemma with him.

I told my therapist about the meeting and Gary Gwilliam, and he just looked at me and said, "Call him, you have nothing to lose." I was astounded. Are you kidding? What would I say?

I did not call men, and I was not looking for a relationship. This was truly crazy.

The next day, I decided to just make the call. I was relieved when his receptionist said he was not in and I was able to just leave a message. What was I going to say, anyway? I was feeling like a teenager, awkward and tongue-tied. You would think I had never dated before.

After playing phone tag for a few days, Gary left his home number so I could reach him more easily. The excuses were running out. I called the number, and he picked up the phone. "Hi Gary, this is Lilly Phelan. I met you at the candle light meeting with Steve Pingle."

"Oh yes, you are Steve's girlfriend."

"Oh, no! We are just friends, and he invited me to the meeting." I then attempted to say again how impressed I was with what he had said, but I was nervous and stumbling all over my words. This was ridiculous, what was I doing?

Gary finally said, "Are you saying you would like to know me better?"

I could have died. "Yes, I guess I do." We ended up talking for a while about ourselves, and he said he would like to know me better as well.

We talked a few times in the next week, and he asked me when I could come up to Oakland. My first response was the week of New Year's, which was about six weeks away. Gary was less than satisfied with this answer, and he encouraged me to visit sooner.

I held firm at first, wanting to postpone this as long as possible, but since my daughter Elizabeth was living nearby in Pleasanton, I decided that perhaps I could go up there sooner so I could visit her. We decided I would drive up on the Saturday after Thanksgiving, which was only two weeks away. I was surprisingly anxious about this date.

As I made my way from Glendale to Oakland, I was still struggling within myself to understand why I was traveling so far to meet a man I hardly knew. In the past two weeks we had talked on the phone a few times about ourselves, our families, and our career goals, but we were still hardly more than strangers.

I distracted myself by thinking about visiting Elizabeth, and seeing her new apartment. She had completed her bachelor's degree at Chico State in 1989 and was now working for an insurance company. Liz was happy to have me see her new place, and we talked about my crazy date. I loved seeing her, but as my date with Gary approached, I found myself getting even more nervous.

As I made my way to Gary's place I missed the exit and got lost, so by the time I reached his building I was flustered and anxious about being a half an hour late. As I walked up to the front of his building and pushed the buzzer to his apartment, he opened the door and welcomed me in to his home. He was as attractive as I remembered him to be. I was unsure how this whole evening would unfold, but I was here now so I decided I may as well enjoy it.

He showed me around his two-bedroom apartment with a stunning view of Lake Merritt. The blue and tan sofa faced the floor-to-ceiling windows, which gave the room a wide open and warm feeling. As I sat down, I noticed that on top of the glass coffee table was a book called *The Journey of the Heart* by John Wellwood. I thought his apartment was comfortable and inviting and found the book on the coffee table intriguing. I was beginning to relax and looked forward to getting to know more about this man. He offered me a glass of white wine while he drank sparkling water, reassuring me that he did not mind if people drank around him, and we talked a while before going to dinner. My anxiety was lessening, but I still felt so awkward.

We went to Skates, a restaurant located in Berkeley, and sat at a window table which looked across to the Golden Gate Bridge and the twinkling lights of San Francisco. Dinner was wonderful and the conversation just flowed between us. Of course, the wine was a big factor for me. He asked if I would like to come back to his apartment to continue the conversation, and since I was feeling more comfortable with him I readily agreed.

Once we were back in his apartment, he put on some Kitarō music and we danced. The music was slow, and I enjoyed feeling his warm body next to mine. I placed my head on his shoulder, his five-foot-ten frame feeling perfect against my five-foot-seven body. I could feel that he was enjoying our dance as much as I was. I pulled back and looked at his light blue eyes as we continued dancing. He then pulled me closer to him, and we kissed passionately. I felt as if I had known him a long time.

He stopped and said to me, "Lilly, I do not know if you will believe what I am about to say to you, but I love you. As we were dancing, I heard this voice say to me, 'This is her!'" We sat back down on the sofa, and he held my hand. "I went to see a psychic last spring, and she told me that my marriage was over, and that I would meet a woman who will be the surprise of my life. And I think that woman is you."

I was totally surprised. A part of me knew that this relationship was something very different from anything I ever experienced in all my years of being single, yet I also knew what he was saying was unbelievable. After all, Gary had left a nineteen-year marriage just two months before. I did not know him, nor did he really know me. How could this be possible? I knew intuitively that he was different than the other men I had dated, but only time would show how true this feeling was.

The view from Gary's apartment was beautiful, and the lights below Lake Merritt were shining bright as we kissed one another again. I was so glad I followed my intuition to contact him; this had been an unbelievable night.

# PART THREE

## Forgiveness

# Chapter 33

### Return to New York

*New York City, 2013*

It felt so strange to be going back to New York to see my mother in the hospital. When I told Carol Ann, my sister-in-law, that I was coming, she offered to let me stay with her and the boys. As much as I appreciated the invite, I declined as I was used to having my own privacy. Besides, I'd much rather immerse my whole self in the energy of New York City. I stayed at the Hilton Hotel on the Avenue of the Americas, which is just a few blocks from beautiful Central Park and two blocks from Fifth Avenue. It was the perfect location for me.

As I walked through this bustling city on my way to visit my mother, I reminisced about the many happy childhood memories from my time in Manhattan. I thought back to when I was eight years old and she took me to the Radio City Music Hall to see the Rockettes' Christmas program. When I entered the hall for the first time, I was amazed by its majestic size. The auditorium was huge, and the excitement coming from the audience was energizing. I still feel that same kind of excitement today when I go to a play on Broadway or walk past the Music Hall. After the show, we went to Rockefeller Center to watch people ice skating and see the lighting of the Christmas tree. Christmas music was playing all around the center, and everyone seemed to be happy.

Often, around this time of year, we would go into the city by train with my mother's two friends and their children, who were about the same age as my brother Sonny. This was a happy time for us, and these trips into Manhattan were a holiday tradition that continued until I was in junior high school.

Walking down Seventh Avenue, I heard the taxi drivers blowing their horns and saw tourists getting something to eat at one of the many vendors selling hot dogs or large salted pretzels. The aromas from the food carts change depending on the time of year. In the winter, I would smell the chestnuts roasting. In the summer, the air would be filled with various foods from the vendors' carts. I especially loved the smell of the warm dough pretzels and the lamb being cooked for kabobs. There were also street vendors selling colorful scarves, hats, and t-shirts that advertised New York City. As I looked into the stores along my walk, I saw tourist shops with miniature Statues of Liberty and small taxi cars for children to play with.

One of the best stores in New York is the Disney Store—it is a child's dream and a parent's nightmare. As I passed by, I saw a mother trying to console her four-year-old boy who was having a temper tantrum about not getting the toy he wanted. He was screaming and falling to the ground, and it made me so glad I was not that mother. I remember those times with my own children, and I am glad they are in my past.

New York City is very diverse. I heard many different languages spoken as I maneuvered myself through the busy streets. There were several employees standing in front of their stores, holding out their cards and shouting, "Come on in! You will get the best deal on this beautiful clothing!" I had long since learned how to dodge them.

There is glamour here, but there is poverty as well. One moment you may see a celebrity walking past you, and the next you are confronted with a homeless person sitting on the sidewalk with tattered clothes that smell of urine, and with a can sitting in front of them, asking for money.

This, to me, is New York, the place I heard about so often from my grandfather when he talked about his love of working in the city, the place I spent many of my childhood years. I would often try to re-create the fond memories of my youth by returning to the rituals and places I loved, but today I was here for a different purpose.

As I arrived at Penn Station to travel on the Long Island Rail Road, I listened to the familiar accents that filled the air around me. I had moved away from New York in my early twenties, and now I found going back home to be both heartwarming and emotionally conflicting. I had always kept my distance from my family, even though I spent years in psychotherapy trying to understand my family dynamics and learning to forgive my parents. At the age of seventy-one, I was still trying to resolve my mother-daughter issues. Now, sitting on the train with the cadence of my family's accent all around me, I could not help but think of my mother, who was in the hospital after a downturn in her health. The harmful comments that she said in my youth had affected much of my life, and I still wasn't sure if I had truly forgiven her. I thought about what I would want to say to her if I knew she were to die soon, which was a very real possibility.

I was jostled from my reverie as the train approached

Massapequa Park. The town looked the same as it did back in the 1950s, when my parents bought their first home here. I got off the train and immediately looked for Carol Ann, and soon I spotted her sitting in her white SUV. I loved Carol Ann. She had a wonderful New York accent and an energetic, positive personality. Her blue eyes always sparkled when we talked, and today her shoulder length blonde hair was curly from the humidity.

On our way to the hospital, we stopped by the house I grew up in and where Carol Ann was living with my two nephews, Jake and Tyler. I had so many memories in this house, and I felt happy to be able to come back here and revisit over the years. It had been a place to ground myself and to measure my growth as a woman. It was also a place of confronting my own mortality—my father and two brothers had all passed away, and four of my childhood friends that lived on this street were also deceased.

My mother was at St. Joseph's Hospital in Amityville, which is one town away from Massapequa. I was relieved that my mother was still alive and that I would have the chance to see her before it was too late, although I was also anxious about how this meeting would go. As we walked down the light green hospital corridor to find her room, a part of me did not want to see her so vulnerable. As we entered her room, my body suddenly became heavy at the sight of her small and fragile body. Her head was leaning to the right side of her pillow with her eyes closed, and her face was sprinkled with white, dry patches which were more pronounced along her hairline. Her thick, gray hair was still short, but it was certainly longer than usual and looked unkempt. I gently touched her shoulder to see if she would wake up, and she slowly opened her dark brown eyes—eyes that did not have the sparkle of life shining in them. She closed her eyes and opened them again, and the sparkle started to come back.

She smiled and said, "You are finally here."

"How are you doing, Mom?"

"I just want to go to the next world," she responded. "I do not want to live like this! My legs have given out on me, and I can no longer walk. I have no control over my bowels, and every time I eat, the food goes right through me. I have to be changed by the nursing staff all the time. All I want to do is sleep." She slowly pushed her blanket to the side of her bed and showed me her swollen legs, caused by her cardiac failure. The skin on her legs was like leather—dry and blotchy, with black and blue marks.

I could feel my chest tighten as she spoke, and I started to cry. I knew it was time to let her go. I sat on the side of her bed and held her hand. "Mom, you know I understand how you feel. If I were you, I would feel the same way. I would not want to live with the quality of life that you have." I leaned in to be closer to her as tears rolled down my face like soft drops of rain. "I will miss you Mom, and I am happy we had a good relationship with one another the past few years."

Having a good relationship was relatively new to me and my mother, although a good relationship in our family was simply one where no one shut the other out and both people said what was true in their own hearts to one another. Yes, I had issues with my mom, but it did not mean that I could not forgive her at the end of her life.

She looked at me and whispered, "You made me so happy."

In this moment, my ambivalence and annoyance with her seemed to slip away, like the taste of fine wine that leaves you feeling warm and loving. I truly felt that I forgave my mother after not being seen by her all of these years. All the anger and frustration I had felt was gone in an instant. She seemed so frail and ready to cross over to the other world, and I was happy to see her in that state of peace and be in this new emotional place with her. Perhaps we were simultaneously crossing over into the next chapter of our lives, although we had very different destinations.

Celebrating my mom's 90th Birthday in California with her grandchildren and great grandchildren.

Celebrating my mom's 90th Birthday in California with her grandson
Patrick, great granddaughter Ashley, and daughter Lilly.

# Chapter 34

### Letting Go

As Carol Ann and I left the hospital, I felt as if I was smacked in the face with the realization that my mother was going to die. It was hard to believe I was witnessing her wish to let go and cross over to the other side.

This experience of losing my mother was so different than the loss of my father and my two brothers. I'd lost my father in 1982 at the age of sixty-four. In 2000 my brother Sonny died at fifty-six years old, leaving behind his adult daughter Angela, and in 2008 my brother Guy passed away at forty-eight, leaving behind his eight- and four-year-old boys Jake and Tyler. The men all died of a sudden heart attack, leaving me with no opportunity to say goodbye. Luckily my relationship with my father and brothers were complete when they passed, so I have felt no guilt about this nor do I feel I left anything unsaid.

Guy's passing had been particularly hard. I was living in California when Carol Ann called, hysterical and overwhelmed, to inform me of his death. As the only child left in our family, I had to be the person to call my mother and tell her. My personal pain of my brother's death was compounded with having to break this terrible news to my mother.

In order to help prepare support for her, we arranged to have a close friend and neighbor nearby. I was lucky to have my husband Gary with me, standing by my side as I dialed her number, trembling with emotion. I was very thankful for his presence. After I told my mom the news, there was silence for a few seconds. This was then broken as she screamed, "No! No, no, no! This is not true! It cannot be!"

Her wail sounded as if it came from a dark and painful place, and it was heartbreaking to hear. I could only sob quietly as my eighty-seven-year-old mother tried to absorb this awful news. I was afraid she might have a heart attack herself, and I was relieved that we had her friend come over to be there with her. It was this day that I developed more empathy and compassion for my mother, which made it possible for me to be willing to let her go.

My mother was still mentally sharp and alert, but physically she was slowly shutting down. The doctors had taken her off her current medications, and she had friends and family call her and visit. She was near death, but her body was not letting go.

Not long after my visit with her, the doctor looking after my mother said they could not keep her in the hospital any longer and recommended that she go into a nursing home. There was no going back to her apartment or coming to live with Carol Ann or myself; she needed total care. My mother knew the nursing home she wanted to get into, which was one town away from her friends and from Carol Ann, and we were fortunate to be able to move her into this very nice facility.

After I returned home to California, I called my mother

to check up on how she was doing in the nursing home. She said she was enjoying being taken care of by the nursing staff and seeing her friends. She had four hours of hospice care five days a week, and the hospice staff were wonderful and provided emotional, spiritual, and physical care. She also had a chaplain who came by each week and spent time talking with her about her spiritual needs. I was relieved to hear that she was safe and being taken care of.

With this additional time in the nursing home, we were able to talk about her funeral wishes. Over the past six years, my mother and I had had several discussions about this topic. She originally wanted an elaborate funeral but hadn't done anything to plan it on her own. She talked about having a beautiful casket with a large church service with a priest and inviting all of her friends and family. She wanted to have a large limo procession with her casket that would drive past the old neighborhood where she bought her first home in 1950. She also wanted to have everyone celebrate her life by having a dinner for all attendees at a restaurant in Massapequa. My mother had a small insurance policy that would cover some of these plans, but she thought that Gary and I would pick up the costs for the remainder. Seriously? I asked her what the point was of having a funeral that she couldn't afford and told her I was not willing to pay for it when she had not provided me with any monetary assistance since I graduated high school.

After I said this, my mother was quiet at first. Then she said, "Don't worry about it. I will take care of my funeral."

To my mother's credit, she soon started making monthly payments to the funeral director to cover the costs. She wouldn't be able to cover everything that she wanted, but she ended up having control over her own funeral.

Before my mother passed, I wanted to help clean up the

relationship between her and her three sisters and bring her some peace. My mother and maternal grandmother had a conflicted relationship all their lives, and at the end of my grandmother's life in 1986 they were not speaking to one another. In fact, my mother didn't even inform me of her death until two years later. I always thought this was incredibly sad, and I did not want to carry on this family tradition at my own mother's death. She had not been in contact with any of her sisters before entering the hospital for a variety of reasons.

Gladys, who was three years younger than my mother, lived one town away in Seaford, New York. Their latest dispute had started after my youngest brother's funeral. According to my mother, Gladys was upset with her because she had not been introduced to my mother's friends. They stopped talking for five years, but they reconciled their feelings of anger and hurt when my mother went into the hospital. They talked on the phone, but despite being no more than twenty minutes away and having family who could drive her, Gladys had never come to visit my mother throughout her entire stay in the nursing home.

Joan and Beryl, who lived in Maryland and Tennessee respectively, did not attend my brother's funeral and their sympathy was scant. They were angry with my mother because she voted for Obama, and even after she went into the nursing home, they did not reach out to make amends.

Personally, I had emotionally and physically shut my aunts out of my life as the family drama had been driving me crazy. Now, though, I wanted to take the high road and feel as complete as I could with my mother before she passed away. I decided to reach out to Joan and Beryl to give them the status of her health so they would have the chance to do what was right within their own personal relationship with my mother.

I had not been in touch with them for many years and neither had my mother, so I was unsure what the best way to reach out would be. After giving it a lot of thought, I sat down at my desk and wrote them a letter:

*This letter is to inform you that my mother, Lillian Louise Radziewicz, is struggling with crossing over to the other side. She is in the Broadlawn Manor Nursing Home as of last Friday, and she will begin hospice care this week.*

*She was independent, living in senior housing during the past five years after the sudden death of my brother Guy. I called every week, and my sister-in-law, Carol Ann, has been very active in checking in on her and taking her to doctor appointments. However, it became clear to us in the past five weeks that she is unable to care for herself any longer.*

*She went into St. Joseph's Hospital about three weeks ago with congestive heart failure, a urinary tract infection, and pneumonia. She can no longer walk because of the heart failure, and she requires total care. She cannot get up to sit in a wheelchair due to the pain in her legs. Her body is basically failing her, and she is very tired. All she wants to do is sleep!*

*She is no longer eating or taking any medications. She is in the nursing home that she wanted to be in and is receiving excellent care.*

*I went back to New York two weeks ago to see Mom and to help Carol Ann clean out her apartment and complete all the necessary paperwork to get her into the nursing home. I told her that I would inform all of you of her condition. She is mentally very sharp and has been able to have control of her end-of-life decisions regarding her medical care. She is being given morphine to help keep her comfortable.*

*I have a phone number that you can call and leave a message. The nurse will read back the messages to her if she does not answer.*

*You are receiving this note because I do not have a telephone number for you. I trust that you will all respond to this note in your own way and do what is best for you to be complete with the relationship that you have with my mother.*

*I hope all is well with you and your family.*

I phoned my mother a few weeks after sending the letter, and she happily reported that both Joan and Beryl had called her the day before. They all had a pleasant talk and laughed about old times together. My mother was now able to forgive them for not being emotionally supportive at the time of Guy's death and in the years that followed, and they were once again siblings, sharing this last chapter of her life with peace and gratitude. I was so happy that my mother was able to reconnect with her siblings before she died. My desire for my mother to have peace, love, and a positive connection allowed them to forgive themselves and one another, breaking the cycle and creating a new and loving family dynamic. Change can still occur all the way up until we take our last breath; this is the power of forgiveness.

Guy and me in our last photo together with my godchild Tyler in 2008 - He died a month later.

Guy with his sons' Jake and Tyler

Guy and CarolAnn

Generations of Motherhood

4 generations of women, great grandmother, grandmother, mother and child

Great grandmother, Emily, and mother Liz and uncle Patrick

Lilly with daughter Liz and grandchildren, Emily and Noah.

Lilly with her son
Patrick, and grandson
Benjamin

My niece Angela and me
after my mother's celebration
of life ceremony

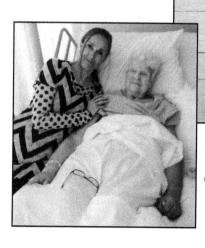

Good-by Mom
I love you

Sonny and his wife Carol, many years earlier connecting with his Mom, dad and brother Guy in heaven in 2014

My children Patrick and Elizabeth are as close together today, as they were as young children

Good bye mom from your daughter and nieces and nephews!
We love you!

# Chapter 35

## I Do Not Love My Mother

Unfortunately, this loving family experience could not last forever; that is not the nature of my mother and her family.

I called my mother at the nursing home at least once a week after she was admitted, and she seemed to be feeling better. One day, as I started to ask how she was, she interrupted me and asked, "Have you heard from Carol and Eddie?" They were the children of Uncle Eddie, my father's youngest brother, and they had come to visit my mother when she first entered the nursing home.

A little taken aback, I responded, "No, I do not hear from Carol unless I call her to get together for a family brunch when I am visiting New York."

"Last Easter they came by and took me to dinner. I thought they would come and see me again this week."

"Mom, Carol is too busy with Eddie right now. He lives an hour and a half away from her. She spends six hours each weekend picking him up for an overnight stay and bringing him back to the nursing facility, not to mention that she still works full time as well. It was really gracious of them to come and spend Easter Sunday with you the past two years when you were living on your own, but now Carol has to drive an additional hour and a half to visit you. She does not owe you anything." As I was telling my mother this information, I felt an anger rising within me at her sense of entitlement. My mother had a way of asking questions like this with the attitude of an expectation, not a request.

As I spoke, she abruptly interrupted me and shouted, "What do you want from me?"

Instantly, I was seething. All my childhood, I'd felt alone, unsupported, without encouragement. She did not want to see me succeed in life, and I was made to feel guilty for wanting more in life than she had. I am ashamed to say that I yelled at her. "I want nothing from you! I have never, ever, gotten anything from you, and had to get everything I have on my own without your help. I have given you thousands of dollars over the years and flew you to California several times so you could see your grandchildren and great grandchildren. The gift you gave me is that I do not owe you anything!"

There was silence on the other end of the phone.

"I will call you next week," I said, and I hung up.

I felt so upset and out of control after this conversation. I was not the person I thought I was, nor was I who I wanted to be.

I was surprised at the strength of the negative emotions towards my mother that still resided within my body, even now at seventy-two years old. What happened to the positive spiritual feelings that I felt when I thought she was dying? I had truly felt this beautiful letting go and forgiveness when I saw her in that hospital bed. As much as I worked so hard on resolving this issue in therapy, I guess I only knew about these emotions when they were triggered once again. Perhaps she's survived this long in order to give me the chance to fully cleanse the anger, guilt, and resentment that had accumulated over my lifetime.

I felt I had a responsibility to myself to resolve these issues with my mother so that I could fully forgive her and myself for the feelings that lingered before her death and find a place of peace in my soul. Instead of calling the next week, I made one more trip back to New York. I sat with my mother and talked to her about my life, the same way I had talked to Liz in that diner. I told her about my childhood, about the ways that she had hurt me and the ways that I had healed myself. My mother listened to everything I said, and she apologized for everything.

As we talked, I finally felt the anger within me release, and I knew that I had found the peace that I had been searching for.

On December 8, 2014, I received a phone call from the head nurse who told me my mother was going to die very soon. She was unconscious, her breathing was shallow, and she was being given morphine to keep her comfortable. I called to speak with the hospice nurse, and she said my mother knew I was on the phone but was only semi-conscious and did not want to talk to me. She told me that my mother said she loved me, and I told her to tell my mother I loved her as well. The nurse told me that her sister Gladys was admitted to the same nursing home a week before but had been placed on another floor. The nursing staff had arranged to have her sister there at her side in the final end stage of her life, for the final goodbye.

My mother crossed over the following morning on December 9, 2014. I knew in my heart that she was now in peace and felt a sense of relief that it was over. Despite all of our conflicts over the years, I would miss her, and I am glad that we were finally able to come to a place of forgiveness and acceptance.

❀

# Conclusion

We are brought up to love our mothers, and for many years I felt guilty that I did not feel this way. It took years of therapy for me to learn that it was okay not to feel this love, and that I needed to forgive my mother for the pain I felt that she did not support me when I was a vulnerable teenager and young adult. But first, I needed to forgive myself.

Through a long process of self-analysis and a determination to not pass on my own family dysfunction, I was able to move away from the example set by my mother and grandmother and create a better relationship with my own children. While I won't pretend that I was always the perfect parent, my children have grown into strong, independent, wonderful adults who have forged their own paths, so I feel that I must have done something right.

In 1995, Liz graduated from Adelphi University in New York with a master's degree in social work at the age of twenty-eight, and she is now a licensed clinical social worker at a medical center in California. She has become a leader in her field and is well liked and respected by her peers. She has a strong work ethic and loves what she does in her profession, and she is a role model for her own children—Emily, age seventeen, and Noah, age fifteen. I am so proud of her and the beautiful woman she has become, both inside and out.

After Patrick received his master's degree in business administration from New York University in 1992, he became the chief financial officer of a community bank in California. Patrick is a very self-possessed and independent man who is not only respected by his professional business peers, but is also a kind, compassionate, wonderful, loving father of two children—Benjamin, age thirteen, and Ashley, age eleven. I am so proud to call him my son.

My children and I continue to have a close relationship to this day. We spend holidays and birthdays together, go on family trips, and enjoy one another's company. I am especially very close with my grandchildren, having spent one day a week with them throughout the early part of their lives. This time was invaluable in creating the strong relationship we have today and can never be erased. I love being a grandmother more than I could have ever imagined, and I am so proud of the beautiful persons they have all become.

I am proud and happy to see Patrick and Liz continue to be close to one another emotionally as well as physically, and as a result their children are very close to each other as well. Being able to see the strong and loving family legacy that I had hoped to create for my children and grandchildren come to fruition gives me a sense of joy, love, and peace.

This memoir has covered my life up until the time I met Gary Gwilliam, and there is much more to my story—too much to include in just the one book. I will be writing another memoir to share the events and lessons of the second half of my life.

I hope that this book has helped you recognize the

generational dysfunctions that can pass down from a mother to her children, and that it has helped those of you with your own challenging relationship with your mother come to a place of forgiveness. There is no perfect answer to make this happen, since each relationship will have its own angst to resolve, but remember that it is never too late to change. Believe in yourself and follow your dreams, and you will come to a place of peace and forgiveness in your heart. This is what makes life worth living.

# Biography

Lilly A. Gwilliam has held a variety of positions over the course of her life. She has been a medical legal consultant and served as the dean of allied health and the accreditation officer at Antelope Valley College. She was the nursing coordinator and a nursing faculty member of the UCLA Neuropsychiatric Institute in California and also worked as a practitioner teacher at Rush University in Chicago. She also held a position as a psychiatric nurse on a surgical unit where she helped patients, families, nurses, and students deal with death and dying.

Lilly was inducted into the nursing honor society, Sigma Theta Tau. She was nominated as one of the "Outstanding Young Women 1979" and is a member of "Who's Who in American Nursing." Lilly has published several articles on the topics of nursing and law and has presented many seminars, including "The Elimination of Gender Bias in the Legal Profession." She presented a paper on rape to the Fiji Law Society and helped change the laws on rape for women in Fiji. She was also inducted into the 2014 Massapequa High School Hall of Fame in recognition of her commitment to excellence as she honors her responsibility to her family and her community.

Lilly currently lives in Alamo, California, with her husband Gary Gwilliam. They have five children and eight grandchildren between them, and they enjoy spending time with their families.

# Contact Lilly

Published Author/Medical Legal Consultant

**Website:**
www.lillygwilliam.com

**Email:**
lilly@lillygwilliam.com

**LinkedIn:**
www.linkedin.com/Lilly A. Gwilliam

**Facebook:**
www.facebook.com/Lilly Ann Gwilliam

**Instagram:**
@lillygwilliam

CPSIA information can be obtained
at www.ICGtesting.com
Printed in the USA
FSHW010033080619

9 781733 899703